Dear April,

SO THAT'S why I keep doing this!

Thanks,

Jean Fetterolf

May 2004

52 DEVOTIONAL STORIES OF ENCOURAGEMENT & INSPIRATION FOR YOUTH WORKERS

So THAT'S why I keep doing this!

GLENN PROCOPIO

Youth Specialties

ZondervanPublishingHouse
Grand Rapids, Michigan
A Division of HarperCollinsPublishers

So Thatʼs Why I Keep Doing This! 52 devotional stories of encouragement and inspiration for youth workers

Youth Specialties Books, 1224 Greenfield Dr., El Cajon, CA 92021, are published by Zondervan Publishing House, 5300 Patterson Ave. S.E., Grand Rapids, MI 49530.

Library of Congress Cataloging-in-Publication Data
Procopio, Glenn
    So thatʼs why I keep doing this! : 52 devotional stories of
  inspiration & encouragement for youth workers / Glenn Procopio.
      p.   cm.
  "Youth Specialties."
  ISBN 0-310-22456-X
  1. Church group work with youth—Meditations. 2. Procopio,
  Glenn, 1957- . I. Title
BV4447.P75 1998
242ʼ.69—dc21

                                       98-7636
                                          CIP

Edited by Lynda Stephenson
Cover and interior design by Jack Rogers
Cover photograph by Jim Whitmer

Printed in the United States of America

99 00 01 02 03 / / 10 9 8 7 6 5 4

To my wife Rhonda.
The morning sun is dim compared to my love for you.

Contents

Preface 9

We Lost a Kid Today 10

Not Quite Desperate Enough 12

A Day to Build a Lifetime On 14

Caught in the Whirlwind 16

A Place to Belong 18

Broken People and the Biltmore 20

I'm Going to Kill My Parents 23

Wall Outlets, Bailing Wire, and the Mickey Mouse Club 26

Lessons I've Learned from My Son 29

The Secret Place 32

Weary Well-Doers 35

The Portrait 38

Nightmares 41

Stuck 44

Portraits in Prayer 48

Turnkeys 52

The Art of Listening 55

A Lesson from Mount Moriah 58

Stretching 61

Do You Think They Get It? 64

Hold On 67

He Must Increase, I Must Decrease 70

Surviving When You've Blown It 73

A Youth Pastor Lived in Buchenwald 76

When God Changes Your Name 79

Zaccheus Speaks 82

192-10 84

Torture 87

Spit, Sight, and Appreciation 90

"Whose Kids Are These Anyway?" 92

A Father to the Fatherless 95

Hidden Worlds 97

Reflections in the Wall 101

Sailing on Ships That Will Never Return 104

The Legacy 107

Destiny 111

Runaways 114

I Feel Like a Used Pair of Shoes 118

Turf Wars 121

Moved by the Word 124

Staff Confessions 128

Great Grace 132

On Arms 136

The Price of Pride 141

Nursing Your Wounds 144

Storm Survivors 148

The Power of Fun 151

"I Wanna Go Wif You"—A Longing for Connection 154

Seeds of Change 157

Dark Clouds, Bright Hopes 160

God of My Emptiness 163

A Word to the Enemy 166

Preface

Do you ever see slide shows when you close your eyes at night? I mean, does God ever turn the insides of your eyelids into twin screens and begin showing you the faces of kids whose lives you're trying to touch with the gospel? When I first started out in ministry, I would never have dreamed that, 18 years later, I could still be so overwhelmed by a teen in need or so intimidated by a seventh grader with an attitude. I would never have dreamed that working with kids would continue to challenge my creativity, burden my heart, and consume my soul.

This book is the culmination of a four-year process that chronicles my sixteen-year journey (thus far) in full-time youth ministry. It's not a thesis, it's the echo of my heart. During times of struggle I often found myself turning to books by Max Lucado and, finding strength there, I'd think, "Man! I wish there was something out there that was written specifically for people in youth ministry." So I began writing down my thoughts. I'd reread them during intervals of dryness. My wife Rhonda prompted me to submit the first couple of vignettes—and kept encouraging me through many rejections.

My passion for kids remains the deep cry of my heart. I'm still involved with a group of teens who keep my knees to the floor and my spirit filled with wonder as I see God working in their lives. It's my hope that these words will be an encouragement to fellow sojourners whose hearts are also sold out on making Jesus more real to young people.

We Lost a Kid Today

I walked into the bank that morning, excited, thinking about the afternoon youth group meeting to begin in just a few short hours. We had new programs, new kids, a great staff, visitors were coming regularly—things were going great. But then as I deposited my check, I spotted a parent of one of our kids. Pam worked at the bank and her daughter, Hillary, had given her heart to Christ a couple of months before. Hillary was shy, but I thought she'd made some new friends at our winter retreat and was solidly into the group.

Wrong assumption. My conversation with Pam was a blow. Hillary wasn't coming back. This shy kid was desperate to belong, to make new friends, but with all the kids we had coming each week, she couldn't find even one new friend. The teen who invited her to the meetings consistently left her alone after they arrived, spending time with other friends and leaving Hillary feeling out of place. The staff helped but Hillary needed peers.

When I returned to the church, my office seemed lifeless. I slumped into my chair and began banging away at the computer keys. The result was something that I shared with my volunteer staff and, later on, the teens.

We lost a kid today.

She wasn't exuberant. She wasn't the school's most popular student. She didn't have a smile that would cause the boys to swoon and the girls to envy. She didn't have a laugh that was contagious.

So we lost her.

The fact that she's missing won't be a particular blow to the group. She was so quiet that hardly anyone noticed when she was there. She was one of the myriad of faces that we come into contact with each week, each one craving something that all want—a place to call her own, a place about which she could say, "This is my youth group." She longed for a place to belong and she didn't find it.

So we lost a kid today.

We didn't lose her because of our facility, nor did we lose her because the leaders weren't adequate. We didn't lose her because we had the wrong message. The message was right; the gospel is powerful, and it was here that she heard the good news, learned of Jesus and met him. It's just that, when the praying was done, and the tears were dried, there was no one she perceived who cared about her enough to keep on praying and keep on caring after the meeting was over.

What she saw was a pegboard with holes of various shapes and sizes except for one her shape, her size. There was no friend to tell her that each hole is custom-cut for the individual. We lost her because she didn't find something she desperately needed, something we, as fellow believers, are supposed to supply. We lost a kid today. For as she looked into the eyes of all those coming and going, she didn't see the love of God for her there.

She was seeking someone who would call her "friend," not just out of politeness but real friendship, a kinship that comes from knowing Jesus.

We lost a kid today. Her name was "Jesus."

"...I tell you the truth, whatever you did for one of the least of these brothers of mine, you did for me." Matthew 25:40

The following week Hillary was back, and this time, surrounding her were teens who had caught a glimpse of their calling—to love one another as Christ loved us.

We found a kid today. ♡

Not Quite Desperate Enough

"**I** don't know, Glenn, I'll have to think about it." The words hurt. Steve was 20 years old. One of our own. And an alcoholic.

He'd been sleeping in his car for the past couple of weeks in the church parking lot. Though he was the homeless one, I was the one upset and frustrated—frustrated because help had been offered to him time and time again. Jobs. Places to crash. Hot showers. Food. Counseling. Prayers and more prayers. And more than a few tears, too.

He sat across from my desk that Monday afternoon and I was offering him help, again. Real help. Tangible, "change your life" stuff. I felt more positive about this time because the church had agreed to pay for the entire year of treatment, more if necessary. And his response was: "I don't know, Glenn, I'll have to think about it."

I couldn't believe it. It's not like he had a lot of options. His family loved him but couldn't trust him for fear of his stealing. His 20-year-old eyes reflected a hollowness, a life controlled by an addiction. Despite several tries on his own and several spiritual commitments, his problem was out of control. I was offering him a veritable banquet of answers from a church who loved him, a church who wanted to see him whole. I offered him a chance at life—and he politely turned me down.

I wept as he left because I could see where his life was headed. I hurt for God who loves him much more than I possibly could. I know it sounds audacious, but that day, I believe the Trinity wept through human eyes.

But there was another reason for my grief that I couldn't shake, a reminder from the enemy that I was a failure. I could almost see him rubbing his hands in glee. After all, I couldn't even give my help away to a drunk. For a moment I felt utterly useless.

Why do I do that? Why is it that when someone under my scope of influence chooses a wrong direction, I take it as a personal failure? Then comes the battle over words not said, things that could have been done, all the while feeling the enemy's oppressive weight of guilt.

During these times of raw hurt, we gaze into the stuff of our souls, and we see for a moment what God sees continually. I came to the realization that it's not about me and how effective I am, that even my best efforts are pointless without the truth of the cross. But I also came to know that, in being rejected, I can identify with the Christ who died for me. In some mysterious way, by grieving for a lost soul, I become more like him.

Bottom line? I have two choices: Give up and go back to a time when service was safe, when feelings were guarded, and when my heart was never trampled. A place where life was predictable and Jesus was small. Or use that pounding ache to be reminded that God has placed me in the position of feeling his pain, of thinking his thoughts and, in the process, stepping a bit deeper into his presence.

Two options, neither without its pain.

I don't know, God, I'll have to think about it.

"Be strong and courageous. Do not be terrified; do not be discouraged, for the Lord your God will be with you wherever you go." Joshua 1:9 ♡

A Day to Build a Lifetime On

As I write this, it's the day after. Yesterday was a day that lifetimes are built on. I had awakend to the sounds of my four-year-old giggler looking for one of his favorite toys. Work was piled high on my office desk, but that was at the church—out of sight, out of mind. Rhonda had taken the two older guys to school and would be shopping the rest of the day. That left me with Jared, the Kool-Aid lover who has captured my heart, and most of my pocket change.

So we jumped on the day. For breakfast, we played a game of Candyland over Cheerios. (He won.) Afterward, he curled up in my lap, and we watched "The Fox and the Hound" while snuggling under the afghan. Then it was off to the mall. We were inseparable. For eight hours he had my undivided attention. If there were a time I loved him more, I certainly can't remember it. The entire day was filled with wonder as the image of a father was being shaped.

We arrived home to the rest of the brood. My son Jason, 13-year veteran of planet Earth, filled me in on his day. Jeremy, a package of pure mischief beginning his ninth season, was tumbling off the couch, while Jared brought Mom up to speed on the "special day with Daddy." It was noisy confusion, mass chaos, mild hysteria. In a couple of words, it was pretty awesome.

Rhonda and I finished the night with dinner. Nothing fancy. Just good food, close companionship, and soul-sharing over coffee.

Last night I fell in love—again.

As I looked into eyes of this one who knows me so well, but loves me anyway, my perspective became a lot clearer, and I realized that I had missed a hundred such days in the name of doing God's work. For a moment I was ashamed.

I have one shot at this life. There are no "do-overs." While God's grace abounds, every day I see realistic reminder of life's brutality: Twelve-year-old mothers, murderers who aren't old enough to drive, kids trying to cope when it hurts just to be alive. If I don't influence my family, you can bet someone else will. If my values aren't passed on to my children, then there are a thousand other voices clamoring to be heard— and they will be, with tragic results.

The lion's share of student ministry is the ability to "read" kids, to pick up warning signs while hanging out, to be able to read the silences that are cues to deeper problems. It's wisdom not found in a book. It's wisdom that comes with a calling, to ministry or parenthood. If I intend to keep this clarity, then I'd better apply this ministry wisdom to the ones God has deposited in my house—to the Kool-Aid lover, the veteran, the mischief-maker, and their mother.

I'm back in the grind. I've spent two hours in two different high schools, and one hour counseling a troubled collegian, just doing what I love to do, trying to get a handhold in the lives of kids. But on my desk is a card that I've just written to my wife (she'll probably cry) thanking her for making us a family and reminding a middle-aged youth pastor of what's most important.

The months ahead are going to be grueling and busy and exciting, the kind of schedule of which burnouts are made. The temptation to slip into the old groove will be alluring, but I've learned something important about myself. The only time I'm *really* happy is when I'm fulfilling my *entire* calling, to a generation of teens—but also to the next generation of Procopios.

I can't wait to get home. ♡

Caught in the Whirlwind

Ever been in a tornado? I have. I'm not talking about a weather condition. I'm referring to a swirling mass of stuff to do that demands your time—meetings to plan, kids to see, high schools to visit, practices to handle, problems to solve, and the list continues. On and on it goes, spiraling down further and further until you're caught in a screaming vortex from which escape seems impossible. And the pity is that no one seems to know that you're there, except you and, hopefully, your family.

What do you do when your list of "To Do's" are scheduled into the 21st century? How do you fight against the whirlwind and still keep your sanity? What can God say to me when I am so busy that my thoughts wander from him even when I pray? How am I supposed to handle all the "stuff" I have to do and still have the time to disciple a teen in trouble?

While the answer is simple, it's never easy. It's a matter of forcing myself to *forget*—and then *remember*.

Bringing every thought into captivity is a major task. In our world, we've been conditioned to respond at a rapid rate to different priorities, and ministers set their pace by this world they're called to serve. But God's calling on my life is not to "busyness" but to servanthood, beginning first with serving him.

That's what Jesus did.

When the heat was up, he went off to be alone with his father, and it was there that he *chose* to forget the pressure of the calling, the tension of the moment, and remembered. He remembered why he was here, who his father really was, what the result of finishing the job would mean, and when he would once again rest with God.

There are times I have to force myself to forget that I have six thousand things to do with only 20 available spaces on my "To-Do" list, and that I have parents and kids all screaming for my attention to their problems. Sometimes I have to force myself to forget that I am in ministry, even if just for a moment, and during those times I remember.

I remember that before this world was formed, God knew my name. I remember that the essence of who I am was determined by the Father before I was conceived and as I was being formed, he chose a unique course for my life. I remember that I am his most precious creation, not only making me, but reclaiming the right to my soul by sacrificing his own Son. It's a humbling experience.

But don't forget to remember.

Remember your first encounter with the Master, and how meeting him personally altered every part of your personality and would forever direct your destiny.

Remember your first experience dealing with a teenager and how the look in those young eyes would consume you with the desire to change a generation.

Remember also that your effectiveness in ministry is directly impacted by the depth of the friendship you have with the one who called you. An old song, "Draw Me Nearer," speaks of friendship with Christ in very poetic terms.

"Oh, the pure delight of a single hour that before thy throne I spend / When I kneel in prayer and with thee, my God, I commune as friend with friend."

God wants more than sweat from us. He wants us as well. He wants to share every waking moment as a partner in our lives. His heart's desire is to constantly remind us of our higher purpose, of a more excellent way, of a life where joy is not the exception but the everyday. And when he is first, there's always enough time to do what's most important. His heart is saddened when our lives are consumed with tasks for him that don't include time with him.

What was it I had to do? I don't remember. ♡

A Place to Belong

For the most part, growing up in an orphanage wasn't so bad. The kids there, including my brothers, my sister, and myself, didn't seem to realize that we were any different from other kids—that is, until the holidays rolled around. It was then that we received a raw reminder that we had no real family. But there is one particular season that thrives in my memory even today. I find myself reflecting back on it regularly, for it was then that I learned what selfless love was.

All of us at St. Peter's orphanage had secret dreams of being part of the perfect family at Christmas—waking up on Christmas morning with all eyes on us, opening presents, eating turkey, playing with brand-new toys. Well, one year the dream came true for me.

I don't remember the couple's names, but I remember every other detail of that magical weekend. A man and a woman opened their home to a six-year-old boy for a season, and in the process showed him what the word *family* really meant. I remember loading into the back seat of their station wagon where a puppet was waiting for me. I still hear the man's gentle warning to keep my hands inside the window and to buckle up. That night I had my first "big" hamburger, and I devoured it as we assembled a model plane together. I remember the smell of the woman's hair and how it felt when she reached her arms around me and pulled me into her lap. It was soft and warm and comfortable. I even remember their dog, Duke, a big boxer with a permanent drool who slept by my bedside.

And when Christmas morning came, I was the center of attention. For that weekend, I was the object of their focus. They loved me and kept on loving me all weekend. I was included in everything, even the smallest tasks. And the last night, all four of us (the dog, too) cuddled on the couch, watching television.   For three days, I belonged. I really belonged.

The ride back was quiet. It was cold outside, but the sun was hot on my face as I sat between the two of them. I remember her wiping a tear from my cheek as we said goodbye, the feel of his whiskers as he gave me one last hug. A few sniffles, a wave, and it was over.

Awesome memories. Wonderful. Lasting. Powerful. When I found Christ, you want to know which memory came racing into my mind?

That's right. This one. I belonged, I really belonged. Those memories kept a lasting impression of how it feels to belong burning in my heart, giving me a goal to shoot for as my wife and I raise our own children.

I wish I knew their names, I wish I had some way to thank this couple (who are probably now in their sixties) for giving a lonely little kid a perfect picture of what it means to be part of a family. God used their lives to remind me of him and what it means to *belong*.

Oddly enough, in the battle for the lives of young souls, there are times when, even a youth minister forgets that we all belong to a family whose borders go way beyond the ordinary. I belong to a family whose Father controls the elements and gives life to every living thing, who ordains the movement of the heavens but still turns a listening ear to my cry, knows the burden I carry for that one rebellious teen, knows my apprehension as I approach kids ready to make a wrong turn in their lives, knows my battles that no one sees. Every day, he presses me to my limits so I will discover that he has none. He shakes me to my core so I might discover he is unshakable, and he gives me innumerable opportunities to love, because I have experienced his love.

These are the times that he encourages my soul, pulls me close to his heart, and reminds me that—

—*I belong.* ♡

Broken People and the Biltmore

Something awesome's about to happen. That was what the look in Shauna's eyes told me, and under my breath, I whispered a prayer for wisdom. I had taken a group of middle-class kids from the Pacific Northwest to east Los Angeles for an inner-city mission experience. We had spent that afternoon at the old Union Gospel Mission building, working and touring the facility.

Outside the building hundreds of people lined the alley, and there they lived, in boxes, under plastic tarps or anything else they could find. The air was scented with cigarette smoke and urine. All around us were the sounds of hurting humanity—different voices, different languages but the same message of hopeless desperation.

Needless to say, the kids were more than a bit affected. Our mealtime was a bit quieter, the conversations less frivolous, and at that point, I was pleased. *This is having a real impact*, I thought to myself.

Major understatement. After dinner, our guide drove us on an eye-opening tour as the homeless prepared for another night on the streets. One family was busily cleaning off their section of sidewalk, others huddled around fire barrels, and still more were already lying down, talking to their "neighbors." Our van was filled with emotion, and lives became forever changed. Already, unspoken questions showed on every young face. But the night had just begun.

Our tour of the city ended just a few blocks over at the Biltmore Hotel. The Biltmore is one of L.A.'s most glamorous and prestigious establishments, hosting stars and dignitaries on a regular basis. From ceiling to floor, it was ornately carved and intricately painted with huge chandeliers and expensive furniture—*the* place to be for the wealthy.

The teens were blown away by the two extremes. They were asked to look around and report back to me and our guide. The idea was to somehow process what they saw here in comparison to what they just witnessed on the streets. My hope was that each kid would experience an inner conflict, one that would motivate them to some sort of caring action.

Shauna was standing by herself in front of one of the many shops staring into her reflection. As I approached, I could see that she was on the verge of tears. "This is getting to you, huh?" I said. That was all it took. At that moment, I realized how special my calling was. I was witnessing what some wait a lifetime to see: a human heart being molded.

She kept repeating, "I don't understand, Glenn, I don't understand." What she was saying was reflective of what was happening inside. The inner battle that Shauna experienced—feeling both grateful and guilty for what she does have, and feeling angry over those forced to sleep on the street when hundreds of empty beds were within walking distance—transformed her. Confusion, desperation, empathy, and sympathy were all a part of her tears. Shauna was hooked—hooked on servanthood.

There are times when I complain about my ministry. The long hours, the lack of appreciation, blah, blah, blah. But at that moment, you couldn't have paid me to be anywhere else. Not many nine-to-fivers ever have such days. I was honored to be there.

Oddly enough, for all the love he has for his followers, Jesus is keen on putting us in situations of inner conflict. He is constantly looking for openings to show us how needy we really are. Just ask Philip.

"When Jesus looked up and saw a great crowd coming toward him, he said to Philip, 'Where shall we buy bread for these people to eat?' He asked this only to test him for he already had in mind what he was going to do." John 6:5–6

Philip looked around for help from the guys, but they were busy looking at the ground or adjusting their tunics, anything to avoid eye contact. Don't you know he wanted to say, "Jesus, why don't you ask Peter? He's great at this sort of thing." At that moment in Philip's mind, faith collided with practicality, and his response in verse nine was, *"Eight months wages would not buy enough bread for each to have a bite."*

The conflict was settled with a miracle. Five thousand were fed with the small lunch of a young boy who gave it all up for Jesus.

Jesus had a plan for Philip—to keep asking the questions until he got it right, to keep asking him to respond by sight until he learned to respond by faith, to keep being placed in an atmosphere of inner conflict until he discovered the secret of inner peace. It's the same plan he has for Shauna, for me, for us all.

And you can bet that he'll never stop making us ask the hard questions, because it's through such times of inner conflict that we discover how very needy we really are, how totally dependent we are upon him for our happiness.

Just ask Shauna. Inner conflict can lead to trust.

Trust always leads to rest. ♡

I'm Going to Kill My Parents

Groggy from sleep, I answered the phone. The message didn't immediately register. The voice on the other end was high-pitched and emphatic. It said again, "You need to get over here, Glenn. I'm standing at the foot of the stairs with a knife in my hand. I'm going to kill my parents."

I was wide awake now.

In another time or place, I probably would have called the police, met them at the house, and tried to minister to the family. But in that split second, something in my heart jumped, telling me that God was wanting to touch Rick.

Of all the kids in our group at that time, Rick was at the top of the "potential" list. He was bright, talented, a gifted communicator with a winning personality. Rick was the type of person everybody loved. But his temper? Scary, really scary.

Rhonda prayed with me before I left, her eyes communicating unspoken concern. I knew this had some dangerous potential. I couldn't quit asking myself one question as I drove the deserted streets to Rick's house: "How about it, Glenn. You ready to die?" Chilling. Spine tingling. But this went deeper than just the standard heeby-jeebies one might expect. This was a foundational question to the root of my being.

As I pulled into the driveway, Rick was waiting on the steps to his house. Two butcher knives lay on the sidewalk. I calmly opened the car window and asked, "How'ya doing, Rick?" He had been crying but he looked at me with a sheepish half-smile and said, "I'm okay now." At that point, I knew that we'd get through the night. Years of resentment, anger, and pride melted in a moment of grace. We talked for a couple hours. I'm not convinced that he would have actually gone through with it, but one thing's for sure, the crisis was enough to scare him into reality. That night was the beginning of the healing process for Rick.

I came home to a warm embrace from a relieved wife. I lay down but sleep eluded me. That nagging question kept replaying over and over in my head, "How about it, Glenn. You ready to die?" The question has stayed around ever since.

I'd like to think that I'm ready for death; that if it came right down to it, I'd be ready to lay it all on the line and do what Jesus did, give his life for others. Wife? Kids? Family? No problem. But what about dying for an idea or conviction? What about dying for a faith that isn't tangible? What about a God I can't see?

During his earthly ministry Jesus consistently taught the principle of self-denial. And scripture is pretty clear that a key to strong relationship with him is being willing to lose your life so that he might live within, losing selfish interests so that kingdom purposes might be enlarged through your obedience. It's an amazing concept when you think about it—God living in all created humans while still preserving their uniqueness and the wholeness of their personalities.

Dying to self these days is difficult to say the least. Many popular examples of modern Christianity seem to emphasize self-promotion rather than self-denial. Others fall prey to the trap of the mundane. Satan has stripped many warriors of their effectiveness for the kingdom by reducing them to armchair quarterbacks, talking tough from the sidelines but not paying the price and entering the fray. But God's voice is constantly whispering to the recesses of everyone's heart, "Are you ready to die?" God's shadow takes in those who have denied themselves to follow a God they cannot see, to trust a faith that is intangible, to live a life that demands their souls, their lives, their all. I want not to be duped into settling for the expected when such greatness is within my grasp.

However, when the decision is made to die to self so that Christ may live within, I have to be prepared. For, in that moment, I make myself an open spectacle to the world. My old nature will scream for attention and, like Paul, I will find that real victory comes only through a daily death, a daily pilgrimage to the cross, where I once again deny myself, take up the cross, and follow him.

Then just like Christ, I may be misunderstood, become the object of ridicule. Radical faith is so profoundly different that it makes many people uncomfortable. Leaders could accuse me of extreme views. Peers might throw up their hands in exasperation over me. Some parents might be afraid of me, some pastors won't hire me. But if I learn how to keep dying, God will reward me with the adventure of a life lived his way, played by his rules, and consumed with his joy.

Because here's the truth. While those who don't know the secret will perceive anyone who makes such a choice as odd and over the edge, kids'll love such a "rebel." Why? Because they're tired of phoniness, of shallow promises from full heads and empty hearts.

Rick and I died together that night. I've died hundreds of times since then.

How about it—are you ready to die?

"And the life I now live…I live by faith in the Son of God who loved me, and gave himself for me." Galatians 2:20 ♡

Wall Outlets, Bailing Wire, and the Mickey Mouse Club

My first experience with grade school was while I was in St. Peter's, a Catholic orphanage in the Memphis area. Thirty years ago it seemed as big as a city to a little boy. During my first month as a third-grader, my teacher, Sister Mary Frederick, made a terrible mistake. She piqued the curiosity of a fearless and inquisitive kid without giving ample warning.

On the particular day in question, we were learning the basics of how electricity worked. I had it all figured out from the get-go. However, in the middle of a fast and furious discussion about what did what and how this worked, the bell rang. Class was dismissed before we got around to discussing what *not* to do.

While the other boys and girls my age were huddled around the television watching the Mickey Mouse Club, I nonchalantly disappeared behind a huge, overstuffed chair, safely out of view from our monitor Atilla, a cross between Julia Child and Bigfoot. I had found a roll of bailing wire, and began fashioning what looked like a wall plug with two prongs. I proudly held up the configuration and realized I had a long length of wire left that I had to do *something* with, so to get it out of the way, I wrapped it around my neck and neatly twisted it together somewhat like an electrical hangman's noose.

I remember looking around to see if Atilla was watching. I remember seeing the wire in my hand. I remember seeing the wall outlet. I remember seeing a *huge* burst of light.

After that, I don't remember anything.

When I came to, all the lights in the entire complex were out and I had four nuns hovering over me. One was crying, one was praying, one was rubbing burn cream on my neck, chin, and hands, and the other was declaring to the world something about someone being incredibly stupid, the last of which I don't remember since my ears were still ringing.

I learned two things that day. One, you don't mess with a power you don't know about. And two, it takes approximately eight hours for those white spots in your vision to disappear.

That day I received a jolt from an unseen power, a charge of energy that I didn't understand, and the results affected a multitude— everybody missed Mickey Mouse that day.

Which brings me to my clever parallel. The same thing happens to those who find Christ, albeit on a wonderfully different scale. They come face-to-face with a power they cannot see or understand, and the results are life-changing for them and those around them. My initial encounter with the power of the gospel was like that.

While trying to get a certain girl's attention, a skinny 18-year-old doper from the south side of Baltimore was tricked into staying all day at an old-fashioned camp meeting. There I was, long hair, wearing a tank top, bell-bottom jeans, and mirror shades (hey, it was the '70s), surrounded by an army of leisure suits (you heard me). Talk about sticking out like a sore thumb. I heard the snickers of the hypocrites when I walked into the service, but I didn't care. The family that invited me seemed to care for me and that made it okay.

Everybody was crowded around the stage and I sat behind a huge overstuffed person, safely out of view of the preacher. The congregation was enjoying a service much like the Mickey Mouse Club of old. There was great music, singing, some spontaneous dancing, and everyone was happy. I wouldn't have been surprised to see Cubby there. It was at that point, though, that I encountered the power of the gospel. I had come for the wrong reasons, but divinity always finds a way to catch humanity offguard.

I remember seeing the preacher. I remember seeing the people drinking in the words which came forth not like a speech but like—well—like life.

Then I remember hearing an invitation to meet God.

After that, I don't remember anything.

That's when I was jolted from the temporal to the eternal, from hopelessness to purpose. God met me there. No payment was expected, no membership roll was signed, I just met him.

Several people were around me, one was praying, one was crying, one man had his hand on my shoulder and kept saying, "You're *his* now, son," while another explained what an incredible display of God's grace I had just received. After all, God had died as my substitute. It was God's power that had drawn me and God's power that forgave me.

That night I learned two things:

• You don't mess with a power you don't understand—you just trust that aching in your heart that draws you to him.

• The joy will never disappear from your soul as long as you're plugged in. ♡

Lessons I've Learned from My Son

Well, it's happened—middle-age. At age 13 my son joined the youth group, and I now have a dual role to play in his life: youth pastor and father. And the first collision came as he was starting eighth grade at a new school in a new city.

We had moved from the Pacific Northwest to the buckle of the Bible Belt and he found it difficult to fit in. Jason is a good guy and makes friends easily under normal circumstances. But he was now the new kid on campus and, as such, was having a tough time. What's worse, he was now getting harassed by a group of eighth grade thug-jocks who were being cruel and abusive. Even at September's See You at the Pole student prayer event, the thug-jocks were there—thanks, ironically, to the Fellowship of Christian Athletes.

That was it. After five weeks, he'd had enough, wanted to quit school, become a monk, join the circus, anything to get out of the situation.

How's a father/youth pastor supposed to handle this one? It was one of those things that consumed my entire being. I'd wake up thinking about him. I'd go to bed with it on my mind. Throughout the day, I'd catch myself wondering what he was doing or how it was going. The mental anguish robbed me of time and creativity. I spent every waking moment hurting for my son who was basically on his own.

The father in me wanted to go up there and protect my offspring (read, "bust a few heads"). But I realized that Jason's relationship with

Jesus would have to become practical. If the faith that I was teaching to the teens in our group was going to work, it had to work for Jason in this situation. The youth pastor in me took over, and together we mapped out a strategy of options—what to do and what to say in scenario after scenario.

The next day, he confronted the entire group of boys, nine in all.

"I, uh, saw you, I think, at See You at the Pole..." He then expressed his dedication to Christ, making them realize they weren't going to get the best of him. Lastly, he challenged them to live up to the example they set around the flag pole that Wednesday morning as supposed members of the Fellowship of Christian Athletes. He was very calm and cool, and honored Christ with his words and demeanor—but he told me later that he was shaking inside.

That afternoon, I picked up a different kid. As I pulled into the school driveway, his head was high, and on his face was a smile that telegraphed a win. He trusted God's way and God honored him. I hugged him and he whispered the words that melt every parent's heart: "Thanks for helping me, Dad." It was a major day. We celebrated that night, just the two of us. He went to bed happy and exhausted and a lot more mature in his faith.

That night as the family slept, I wrote Jason a note. Through a trial in my son's life, God reminded me that he is faithful, and that I could indeed be a father as well as a youth pastor to my sons if I kept a cool head and a focused spirit.

This is what I wrote:

Lessons I've Learned from My Son

Trust is never trust unless it's tried.
Confidence in Christ becomes more real when challenged.
Faith in Christ becomes more real when shared.
The enemy is tinier than he appears.
God is infinitely larger than he seems.
Victory comes to those who dare to trust God's ways.

God comes to those who dare to trust him.
Standing alone is never easy.
Standing alone is always worth it.
Your Father will always be there for you.
In times of hurt, someone else hurts with you.
There's no feeling like being loved.

It took a 13-year-old boy to demonstrate to me that faith and life in Christ works, not just in church but everyday.

And if it works for a scared kid, it can also work for a middle-aged youth pastor. ♡

The Secret Place

Blessed by an abundance of heroes, I've been. Paul Isom, who could play the "Hogan's Heroes" theme on the baritone sax. Sister Mary Frederick, who could crow like a real rooster. Jimmy Pumphrey, who could recite the entire alphabet in a single belch.

Okay, so my childhood criteria for heroes was somewhat limited. Let me tell you about a real hero.

All of his life, Rodney Friend has struggled with personal pain. He was born with a rare retina disease in his eyes known as Sarcoidosis which led to and was complicated by acute glaucoma. Glaucoma is a condition where the pressure inside the eyeball is much higher than normal—in Rodney's case, three or four times higher. He spent the first 18 years of his life in and out of hospitals, being the recipient of experimental medicines, all the while suffering incredible pain. It was during those days that God became real to Rodney.

Every morning, during each stay in the hospital, the first thing he would see was a poster on his ceiling. The poster was in large letters so that Rodney could read it without his glasses. His mother made a new one each time he was admitted. It was the entire passage of Psalm 91 KJV, which begins: *"He that dwelleth in the secret place of the Most High, shall abide under the shadow of the Almighty."* There were times Rodney's pain was so intense that he would scream out, begging for relief. Then he would remember the words, and during those times he would slip into God's secret place where he could trust God's wisdom as well as God's power.

Then, at age 18, God healed him. Flat out. No pain. No problems. No medicine. A touch of the divine to the cries of the desperate. God came through with what seemed to be a true healing miracle.

I met Rodney for the first time 10 years after all of this. We were both employed at a church in Detroit where he was headmaster of the school and I was the youth and music guy. I saw him develop a ministry, fall in love, and get married (I was his best man). Here was a gift named Rodney that God dropped on a congregation. His heart touched a generation of young people and their parents in a way unique only to him.

During his fifth year of ministry, things changed. I remember the morning he came into our school staff meeting holding his right eye and barely squinting through his left. The disease was back and so was his pain, each eye movement communicating a new level of agony. He went to a specialist who sent him to another specialist. The doctor would need to make a hole in his retina with a laser to relieve the pressure.

I have to admit it, I was taken off guard. Rodney's relationship with Christ was everything I wanted mine to be. I was mad at God, bitter, and more than a little confused, because my friend was in such agony.

Rodney had the procedure, was placed back on medication, and the next day came back to work. As we were talking over lunch, he began to tell me how awesome God was, how thankful he was, and on and on and on. *C'mon!* I wanted to shout. I couldn't believe it. Here was a man who had been delivered from a painful affliction for 18 years, only to have it return with a vengeance and he was telling me how good God was.

What I didn't realize then was the secret of the secret place. The reason it's called the "secret place" isn't because it's hidden from everyone. There's no great formula or treasure map that's needed to find it. Nor is it referred to in such terms because it's reserved for only the best or most holy of saints—any one who knows Jesus has an open invitation. It's called the "secret place" because *very few* actually enter it.

What Rodney showed me so vividly was that God's secret place is meant for those who are in need of shelter. The reason he could enter that secret place was because he was so destitute of self that he had nowhere else to turn. So he remembered the words: "*He that dwells in the secret place of the most high, shall abide under the shadow of the Almighty.*" He then entered with nothing to offer Christ but his love and devotion, and God met him there, overshadowed him, comforted him, reassured him of his presence, and reaffirmed his calling on Rodney's life.

As he squinted through his good eye and told me the story, I got it. I understood. And I promised myself that I would enter the secret place, too.

I have many times since.

The secret place is open to all who come before him without pretense, without attitude, but with a life that is poor in spirit, destitute of self, needy of him.

Since that time, Rodney and his wife Carol have been to Romania as missionaries. They had to return home in 1991 because of a relapse, but went back again to Eastern Europe in 1996, taking their secret place with them.

By the way, the promise that Rodney held to all his life is found in verse eight of that same psalm: "Only with your eyes shall you look and see..." ♡

Weary Well-Doers

Neal. A typical '90s church kid. Dysfunctional family. Divorced parents. He's been in church all his life and his experience with Christ could be best described as lackluster.

But something has happened that you need to hear.

You need to hear it, because you have kids just like this one. You need to hear it because one day all your efforts and prayers are going to hit pay dirt.

Neal's had a tough year. He's had to deal with some heavy-duty stuff—becoming a senior, coping with his mom and dad in the various aspects of a split household, and trying to handle Christ's persistent knocking on his heart, to name a few. I'm afraid that the perception of Christianity in the '90s has left not only him but a generation of teens wondering if that's all there is. Is it just a matter of saying a few prayers or crying a few tears? Forgiveness seems to be taken for granted, mediocrity seems to be the norm, and relationship with Jesus changes depending upon how things are going at the moment.

But the cry of the human heart is to have a relationship with God that is something more, something deeper. Something drives us to understand and experience his presence. I've often wondered what made guys like David Brainerd and John Wesley tick. What made their faith so powerful that their influence is still felt today? My guess is they had a faith based on more than what today's Christianity is offering. Their faiths pushed them to moral excellence—they were founded upon truth. They understood "true" truth, and because of that understanding, they were able to stand in difficult times and lead a new country into the Great Awakening.

That's what I've been pumping into Neal the last couple of

months: "When it becomes difficult to stand, stand on what you *know* to be the truth."

We spent time together trying to engrave that truth into his heart, yet I wondered if he was paying any attention at all. On a ministry trip this summer, we had an emotional conversation after he verbally abused another kid, which opened up doors to deal with some more serious internal issues. As long as I was pushing, it seemed he was okay; if not, he kind of fell apart.

So when school started this year, I couldn't help but worry about him a bit—nothing major, you know, just that nagging anxiety that keeps a name or a face at the forefront of your prayers. It's at these times that God, in his unique way, will drop an unseen miracle into your lap. If you're not looking for it, you could miss it entirely.

It happened a couple of weeks ago at our youth group meeting. All the teens were involved in the worship, things went smoothly, and we ended with a call to deeper commitment to Christ. Kids were together at the front, praying, crying, touching the heart of God. Conspicuous by his absence was Neal. I was a little worried that Neal's faith may have gone south for the school year. "Oh no," I thought, "here we go again." But then I looked a bit closer. Neal was there. He was just all the way in the back by himself. Praying, really *praying*. He didn't have to have a staff member there encouraging him to pray. He was sitting there having a conversation with Jesus.

Neal had been listening after all. He didn't need an emotional appeal or a guilt trip placed on him. He responded to what he knew to be the truth.

He's got a long way to go. I know it, and so does he. But some things are different: He has something to stand on that will last when he doesn't *feel like* keep on keeping on; he has something to live by that won't fade during times of struggle; he has a friend in Christ who cares enough to back off the feelings so he can learn to stand and is wise enough to affirm Neal's heart with truth. I'm convinced that Neal's going to make it.

I can't help but think that Jesus had a similar experience with

Peter. Though impulsive and loud, Peter occasionally showed sparks of greatness during the three years that Jesus was molding him. When all others were turning away from Jesus, Peter responded with one such spark. The crowd was leaving Jesus because of his hard words and so he asked the disciples, "Would you also go?" In a moment of soul-searching honesty, Peter responded with words that still resonate to a searching world, "To whom would we go?"

If the "high-five" had been popular back then, Jesus would have raised his hand high for Peter.

Peter responded not with what he *felt* to be true but what he *knew* down deep within. That same central truth also applies to you and me. The only reason our lives make any sense at all is because of Jesus, so where else are we to turn?

Keep pumping kids with the truth. You are close to the heart of Jesus. God isn't blind. He's pleased.

High-five. ♡

The Portrait

Though work began on the painting only twenty or so years ago, the idea was conceived before the world was formed. The Master Artist produced a masterpiece unlike the world has ever seen or would ever gaze upon again.

Greg is a masterpiece.

You wouldn't know it to look at him, but he is. He can't talk. Walks with a shuffle. But his eyes—they communicate a heart for Christ that few will ever enjoy, let alone understand. Greg is a masterpiece, a misunderstood work of art amid the mundane. In a world filled with self-absorbed dreams and shallow realities, he is a model of God's handiwork, a priceless collection of miracles that draws attention to the Father.

A few years ago, Greg was an attender at our first youth group. Don't get the wrong idea—when he was with us, he was an average kid who had identity problems with himself and with God. He was committed to Christ when things were well, but his faith lacked root and when the heat was hot, it showed. Greg was the type of guy you'd always have the serious talks with before, during, and after trips. He was the one that made you shake your head and say, "What's wrong with that boy?" He wasn't a bad kid, just always on the edge of right and wrong, and you couldn't help but like him. The mischievous twinkle in his eye prompted me to excuse a lot more than I should have, and his reluctance to go deeper in his experience with Christ always kept me praying a bit harder for this masterpiece in the making.

Shortly after we left Detroit, Rhonda and I received the news by telephone in horrid phrases—a drunken driver in a pick-up, Greg on a moped, multiple head injuries. One moment he is a carefree kid with a long life to look forward to; the next, a truck mirror catches him on the back of the head, shatters his helmet, and leaves him with a mind that's a vacuum and a body that doesn't work.

We were told that Greg would not survive. But the Artist wasn't finished.

We were told that he'd never come out of the coma. But the Artist wasn't finished.

We were told that he'd never lead a productive life again. But the Artist wasn't finished.

Greg beat all the odds. The first couple of times, everyone shrugged it off: "Man, that guy certainly is lucky." But time after time, Greg displayed the reality of the miracle-working power of God. In a matter of months, he had regained the use of his hands and arms and was beginning to feel his toes again. Greg's memory had been erased and he had to relearn everything, but his mental faculties were all still intact.

His greatest challenge was in communication. His brain had lost the ability to send messages to make his vocal chords operate properly.

He learned the alphabet and some basic words again and began "speaking" with the use of an electronic keypad that allowed him to type out his thoughts. It was then that we fully appreciated the creative love of God. Though Greg had forgotten his family and his language, the one thing he did remember was a friend, a friend he had met in our youth group.

Jesus.

He forgot *everything* else, but the Masterpiece remembered the Artist.

I visited Detroit a couple of years after the accident and Greg was there. He was still in a walker at the time and was learning English enough to communicate in sentences. When I saw him, I was a little apprehensive and had this overwhelming desire to smother him with an embrace, but I realized that he probably didn't recognize me. So I played it cool and just stood before him as his mom began to introduce us.

After studying me for a few moments, he began typing: "*Jesus???*" I shook my head in the affirmative. He didn't recognize me but he discerned a connection to the Master. His mom and I brought him up to speed as quickly as we could and Greg and I had a quiet yet interesting conversation.

One thing had changed in his life in the years that we had been apart. Greg now had a real reason for living. The driving force in his life was the Master. He was the friend of God. He experienced what that old-time gospel hymn "Friendship With Jesus" speaks about:

"Friendship with Jesus, fellowship divine / Oh what
blessed, sweet communion / Jesus is a friend of mine."

His body and spirit both continue to improve. His friendship with Christ grows sweeter, and with each day the canvas becomes more reflective of the Master's handiwork.

May I gently remind you that you're also a work in progress? What you will be has yet to be seen. Everyday the colors change, blending into a portrait of grace, painted by the Master Artist who designed you before creation existed. The circumstances you face everyday are the Artist's tools to produce the Masterpiece of your life. You don't necessarily have to understand his techniques, you don't even have to agree with his color scheme, but you do have to trust. Trust that he does know best. Trust that all you encounter has the potential to produce your good and his glory. When the canvas is done, the portrait will draw those who behold it to the Master Artist.

Wait till you see the finished work. It'll blow you away.

"Dear friends, now are we the children of God, and what we will be has not yet been made known." 1 John 3:2 ♡

Nightmares

My wife and I are both night owls, so it was 1 a.m. when I heard a whimpering coming from the bedroom of my two younger sons. Jeremy, our second-born, is a live wire when he's awake. His eyes are always dancing with mischief and his quick wit makes him a lovable kid.

But as I entered his room that night, I realized he was having a nightmare. His face was contorted with confusion and terror, and just before I got to his bed, he bolted upright, screaming. It was one of those times when you were glad to be right there when your kid needed you. As his eyes slowly focused on me, a priceless look came over his face. Through the dim light of the hall, his teary eyes locked on to mine and a relieved little boy threw his arms around his dad. I hugged him, kissed him, and reassured him that everything was okay. The next 45 minutes, as he fell back to sleep, I was by his bedside, stroking his hair, quietly speaking words of comfort.

Nightmares don't always happen at night. They don't always happen when you're asleep, either. Ask a youth pastor who's been raked over the coals by a parent on the church board. Ask a kid struggling with an area of sin that he can't get a handle on. Ask the father of an AIDS patient or the mother of a 14-year-old gunshot victim. They can tell you that nightmares come in varying degrees of intensity. They can last sometimes for years, and some of them come with no possible hope of ever waking up to a brighter morning when everything will be "okay."

While living in Yakima, each staff member at my church was responsible for one day of hospital visitation each week. One Friday I was making the rounds, spreading some upbeat youth pastor cheer to those in the hospital. Last on my list was Jeanette. Jeanette was in the last stages of terminal cancer, and I wanted desperately to leave her husband Ben with some encouragement while I prayed for his wife. I greeted him as I came into the room and then paused a minute to express my concern. Ben was a mild-mannered, six foot three, 240-pound hulk of a man, and up to that moment I had never heard him raise his voice. But just before I parted my lips to pray, he let me have it!

"Tell me, Glenn," he hissed, shaking, tears welling up in his eyes. "Tell me you believe in God. You look into my wife's eyes, you listen to her delirious babbling, and you tell me that he controls everything. You tell me God loves me when my world's falling apart."

Needless to say I was at a loss for words—surprised by his outburst and overwhelmed. I couldn't bring myself to tell him that I understood, because I didn't.

I just stood there looking into his eyes as he waited for me to answer. Finally, I said: "What do you want me to say, Ben? I don't understand this any better than you. I don't know what to say or do to make it all go away, for Jeanette *or* you. But I can *stay* with you a while, I can *cry* with you, and I can grieve with you." I laid my hand on his shoulder and both of us wept.

I didn't say another word for an hour. The room was filled with quiet sniffles and the heavy aching of two sorrowful hearts. As Ben processed the pain, I was there, and so was Jesus, clothed in the frame of a youth pastor who had learned the practical reality of the biblical words "mourn with those who mourn." For Ben, the nightmare was in full force and God was there by the bedside, stroking his heart with comfort and quietly speaking words of peace. That nightmare day, Ben let go and found his faith again, and no matter what happened, he knew that somehow, in ways he won't be able to explain, everything would be okay again.

God occasionally places us in someone's nightmare, desiring that we might be bedside comforters to a soul desperately needing to know that, with Christ, everything can indeed be okay again. It's a painful place where no theology is offered and no catchy three-point plan of action is given. In that place we "mourn with those who mourn," and we're there to comfort, to reflect the Father's love, and with a confidence that is felt more than told, to help those caught in horror's grip know that there is a hope for tomorrow that transcends every tomorrow we will ever have.

Ministry is more than sharing the words of Christ. It's sharing the essence of Christ as well—his comfort, his love, his peace. Sharing Christ's words are relatively easy, because there is no inherent risk to the speaker. They're not the speaker's words. But sharing Christ's heart? That's another thing, a risky thing, because at that point of hurt, although you may look human, you represent the divine.

Like it or not, although God can use any means necessary to comfort the hurting, he mostly depends upon people like you and me to be channels of his touch. Before we can possibly be used in that manner, we need to be willing to experience Jesus on the most intimate of levels, identifying with his death as our death to sin and self, and identifying with his resurrection as our ticket to a new life in Christ—a new life we're expected to share with others.

Jeanette died a few days later, and at the funeral Ben caught me in the foyer of the church and swallowed me with a massive, tearful hug that lasted more than five minutes. Those who were gathered around waiting for him to finish had no idea what was going on—what connection was there. But I did, and that five-minute hug communicated far more appreciation than a thousand thank-yous.

For at least one afternoon, I had become Jesus—and, for Ben, the nightmare was now over.

"Rejoice with those who rejoice, and mourn with those who mourn." Romans 12:15 ♡

Stuck

Mr. Johnson was a teacher in the local elementary school in Brooklyn Park, Maryland. When my brothers and I were reunited with our father after seven years in an orphanage, Mr. Johnson took a personal interest in us. I guess he kind of felt sorry for the Procopio boys and he wanted to make an impact in our lives. He wanted to show us a good time, and we were excited to go over to his house one fall afternoon. We should have warned him about the cloud that followed us around, but when you're a boy, you don't think about such things.

My four brothers and I jumped out of his station wagon and were ready for fun. He'd raked several huge piles of leaves, and while he started a campfire for the hot dogs, we were jumping from pile to pile. Plain hot dogs burned to a crisp never tasted so good, and we decided to end the day by going into downtown Baltimore to look at the Christmas gardens. In 1966, the department stores in Baltimore displayed magnificent Christmas scenes in their store windows, and crowds would walk the streets going from store to store enjoying the displays. There was no end to Mr. Johnson's patience. He lovingly put up with question after question.

As I reflect back, I know what he was thinking. I know that up to this point, noble thoughts about being there for a group of kids who needed love were going through his mind. It must have been a warm feeling, full of satisfaction, and he must have thought to himself, "This has been a day well spent." That was, of course, until the Procopio boys discovered their first revolving door.

The Hecht Company revolving door was an impressive entrance for any building and unique for two reasons. One was its size (two people could walk abreast in each compartment). Second, other than a small emergency door, there was no other entrance to the front of the store. All the other exits emptied into the alley in the back.

My brothers and I looked at each other. We were impressed. The door was made of gleaming gold and silver and smoked glass, and the soft swishing of rubber against polished metal seemed to call us—to beckon us even: "Come play with me." We could do no less. As we walked through the doors, in and out, faster and faster, an entrance-turned-instrument-of-amusement soon became a game of chance, the object being to get in the door without getting caught between the side of the door and the circular jamb and, once in, to make three speedy laps and keep it going before jumping out and allowing the next crazy Italian a turn.

Mr. Johnson was frantically trying to stop us, but half of us were inside and the other half were outside. Every time he corralled one, the others would be loose. He finally gave up in frustration and decided to let it run its course. He sat on the sidewalk with his feet in the gutter, shaking his head, mumbling to himself.

It was my turn and I was going to keep the game going. I jumped in and just before I reached the other side of the door, the game stopped. The door stopped abruptly. Unexpectedly. Pain shot through my leg and ankle. My foot was caught in the door and I was *stuck*. In times like these it was gratifying to know that my brothers were there for me, empathizing with me, feeling my pain. They disguised their anxiety and fear for my well-being by laughing uncontrollably, but I knew that they were concerned for me. My older brother told me later, "I called the ambulance. I had to. I couldn't breathe!" After two hours, three news crews, more fire trucks than can be counted, and a host of disgruntled shoppers, they dismantled the door and finally got my foot free, a little swollen and purple, but none the worse for wear.

We never saw Mr. Johnson again. We often wondered why.

I've often felt the same way while in ministry. Stuck in a revolving door of time schedules and expectations, rude kids, and inconsiderate parents, frustrated in wanting change to occur, and aggravated when the wrong change takes place. Faster and faster the ministry door spins, until finally, the divine voice is drowned out by an endless turbine of more and more stuff to do with less and less purpose to drive you. And one day you wake up—panic sets in, because you feel "stuck." Stuck in a profession you're having second thoughts about, doubting whether you truly have a calling.

What I had to learn was something no one in Bible school prepared me for—the fact that there are "seasons" of ministry. A cyclical process that continually brings you face to face with why you exist, why you do what you do, and where to head in the future. I'm convinced that many in youth ministry won't last past their fourth or fifth year because no one ever told them about seasons.

No one ever told me that one day I'd wake up and ask myself "What am I doing here?" No one ever told me that working with kids carries an incredible price in rebellious looks, in parents with no understanding, in midnight sobs for that one kid in a hundred who's getting ready to blow it. No one ever told me that a burden for one kid who loathes me could consume every waking moment. No one ever told me that I'd get appreciated so little or be worked so hard.

Seasons for the most part are a series of dark nights of your soul during which you don't truly understand why you're feeling what you're feeling. Confusion seems to guide your life and your "To Do" list reads somewhat like this: 1) Get up. 2) Survive. 3) Go to bed.

Seasons hurt. But if you know that seasons are coming, they can become an ally in your walk with Christ.

You need to absorb these words, for if you've never experienced a season, you soon will.

Seasons come regularly to most people. For some, one comes every two years—for another, every four. It's different for different people, but seasons are regular occurrences where God shakes us up on the inside just a little to keep us ever seeking his direction in our lives. Sometimes they surface because of a personal failure or a test in our ministry, but when these seasons of self-doubt and inner confusion come, they are never without the Father's permission. So take comfort in that. The Father has faith not in how we feel at the moment, but in what we know to be truth. That truth you've been pumping into teens? It works for you as well.

Here's advice to get anyone through the seasons.

Slow down the door. During seasons, it's easier to bury yourself in a flurry of activity that will justify your ministry. Only problem is, it doesn't work. You still lie down at night with the same questions and concerns, only you're emotionally exhausted to boot. Delegate some responsibilities. Say "no." Force yourself to get alone with God. I say *force yourself*, because you won't feel like it. Seasons are like that. But by slowing down you can once again hear the heartbeat of your soul, and you can sense his nearness.

Be patient during seasons. Minutes may seem like years, but rest assured that seasons don't last forever. They are the chisels and hammers God uses to chip away at our exteriors as he searches for the hidden diamond inside. If we are patient, we'll be better for the process. Hold off all major decisions until after God has brought you through and you can confidently step into whatever he has planned for your life. To do less only changes the environment, not the reality or the frustration.

Lastly, use this season to lean on a brother or sister in Christ. Even Jesus knew the value of leaning on a friend during times when seasons were at their peak.

The kids in this world don't need to see another youth worker spin out and leave after getting stuck in a season. They're looking for someone who can press on and get through victoriously, someone who can make it through these seasons and still make it work.

They need someone to show them they can make it—because they have seasons, too. ♡

Portraits in Prayer

What must it be like for God when prayer times are at their peak? It's one of the Supreme Being's attributes that absolutely amazes me—how he can hear each prayer that's prayed and still manage to touch each heart with wisdom and comfort, without ever getting overwhelmed. Heaven is constantly bombarded with the cries of souls sharing a gamut of emotions from the heartache of tragedy to the height of victory, yet God is still able to rejoice and grieve with them all, at the same time.

If we were able to hear the cries of all youth leaders as they prayed one night, what would it sound like? A cacophony of voices raised in gratitude and petition, in anguish and praise, expressing the inmost yearnings of souls needing connection to a supernatural father. What would we hear?

●+●

Wow, what a night! I can't believe that after all these months of walking on egg shells around this kid, he finally made a commitment. He had me scared, Lord. But you came through. I didn't even expect to see him there, I was just grabbing a soda on the way to the game and there he was, sitting in the parking lot, looking like a lost puppy. This kid had hardly spoken to me with more than a grunt. But by asking a 'pat' question, 'How'ya doing, Ken?' he opened up. God, I know it was an appointment set up divinely and I'm grateful for the way you encouraged me, the way you burdened my heart for this kid, the way you kept a picture of his face alive in my head while I was trying to sleep. He's got this bad reputation at school, but he was like every other kid I've ever met who's needed Jesus. And when it really counted, Lord, you found him, just like you found me. Thanks, God, for Ken, for me, for everything. I know the real challenge of discipleship is ahead. Light my way.

Lord, I need your help. I'm not doing so great. On the way to the ski retreat, I caught them both, the deacon's son and the pastor's daughter. Now I've got to face the pastor. I hardly know how to tell him. I know he's a man of God, but sometimes he's so hard to talk to. I'm not sure if he's supportive of my ministry here. And I just don't know how to tell him this. I'm afraid of how he might react and I'm concerned for these two kids who are closer to the edge than they should be. Lord, prepare his heart, and give me words seasoned with wisdom I don't have, or like Philip, move me to Ethiopia—now! Lord, please, light my way.

Father, it's been a long time since I've experienced your nearness like this— too long. Truth is, I didn't really want to come on this retreat. I had other, more urgent things to do. This morning's session was boring. I thought of everything else I could be doing—more productive, more meaningful things. Then Pastor instructs us to have a prayer walk in the woods, alone. Although I had a mental list a mile long, right now I can't think of another place I'd rather be. Because as I grew quiet, you drew near. I've forgotten how beautiful it is here and all of it is your handiwork. From the smallest leaf to the grandest mountain, you created it and, today at least, you created it for me to enjoy. I'm sorry, Lord, because I've relegated you to a mere 15 or 20 minutes between appointments, when you've done so much for me. I'm not content to go back and slip into the same old grind. Something needs to change. I'm going to be quiet now, Lord, and listen to you. As I do, light my way.

Oh God, why did I do that? Sometimes I wonder what I'm even doing in youth ministry. I know Jake's a handful, but he didn't deserve the verbal attack I just gave him, especially in front of everyone. Here I am telling my staff to never correct a kid in front of the group and I do it myself. You'd think that after two years of working with kids, I'd learn to think before I speak. When will I come to the point that I can remain calm

when I'm under pressure? I know Jake loves me and I know that he'll forgive me, but I'm tired of the same old thing happening, God. Help me out, Father. Light my way.

●✝●

It's a boy, Lord. And he looks like me. I can't believe he's finally here. While his mom's sleeping, I wanted to talk to you. He is the coolest thing that's ever happened to me. I can't remember being so happy—or so scared. God, I've always been a mess-up, not in a major way, you know, but I've never quite taken life very seriously. I suppose that's why I entered youth ministry. I've always been able to laugh at life and not really care what others think. But over the last hour, I've realized that life is so important and so precious that I'm not sure that I can do this without messing up. I have kids in my group that have no relationship with their father, and I don't want my child to end up that way. I want to be a great parent, not just a good one. I need your help, Jesus. Light my way.

●✝●

Okay, I've had it. I'm tired of asking for your help. I have prayed and confessed and believed and done all the right stuff. I've tried anointing oil and humble prayers, prayer cloths and healing crusades. And still, my husband is dying. I'm not sure if I can take this. I feel like I'm losing my desire to serve you because I'm so confused. I'm tired, so tired of asking, then getting my hopes up, only to be disappointed again. The teens are watching me. They're waiting to see if I'm real. They're waiting to see if I'm going to break. Well, Lord, I'm ready to break. I don't want to hurt the kids, I don't even know how to pray, I need something from you, but I have no idea what it is. If you care for me at all, light my way.

The prayers find their mark with God, a loving father, an older brother, a trusted advocate:

I share your joy, as a matter of fact, the heavens are even now rejoicing in Ken's newfound faith. I drew him, I redeemed him, but it was your prayers that kept my spirit ever pressing. Your care and concern communicated even through the simplest of questions.

I know it's going to be a tough meeting with that pastor. His distance is a safeguard that he's constructed after years of church battles. Tell him the truth with a broken heart and a tender spirit, and realize that whatever happens, you are never alone. I am guarding your life, and I have chosen you to touch these kids at this time.

It's good to hear from you again, too. I have longed for this time with you for months. Don't you get it? When you are diligent about spending time with me, you are happier. You have more joy and your life is more peaceful. While you are silent, let me embrace your soul with my nearness and help you set some priorities that will truly last.

Jake understands that you are human, and that we all occasionally have bad days and blow it. Use this failure as a tool to change, to reflect my image, to let my spirit make you more like me. And understand that as long as you live on earth, I will constantly be bringing you face-to-face with your inconsistencies so you will learn to depend upon me.

That's quite a little guy you have there. I've been waiting for nine months to see that look on your face, that "new father, happy and proud but scared stiff" look that all you guys get. Every new parent is afraid of blowing it, but you're beginning this little fella's life off right—talking to me. As long as you treat him as he is, a gift from my hand, you will do fine. This is not a time for fear, but for soul-searching, for prioritizing, and for asking yourself, what things in my life are really most important? The answer to that question is in your hands.

I heard your sobs last night, even before they were articulated into a prayer. I know how you're feeling, and I know what it means to watch someone you love die. I know you want definite answers now. You want to know if he is going to live or die, and you see me as cruel for not giving you an answer. But in the midst of your pain, remember that I have a plan that is circular, what is good for you is good for him, and all others involved as well. You have helped teens trust in my power. Now it's time for you to trust in my wisdom as well.

I heard your prayer, every prayer. And I'm lighting your way. ♡

Turnkeys

His father's advice was, "If you don't take care of him, I'll take care of you when you get home." So he went to school that day, his mind dulled by fear and his father's beer. Dad and his cronies watched from the back of a pick-up truck as he brandished a knife during the big fight—and when it was over, George was left there, alone, listening to the gurgling of a dying 17-year-old gasping for his last breath. George watched him die, then waited as the police arrived. His father was nowhere to be found.

George was a kid in our Yakima group who came maybe twice before his family moved out of town. Although not a bad kid, he was always troubled and could never get a handle on really knowing Jesus, let alone serving him. Part of the problem was his wigged-out family—a drunken dad and a battered mom. George never listened to counsel, mine or any other leader's, nor did he respond to any love shown him. I'd see him every year at youth camp. He'd hang out but he'd never commit. He was always nice, always quiet, but definitely not the type you'd think would make an impact on his world.

But he did.

At his school, he'd had an altercation with another student that escalated into a big deal. His classmates were watching him, trying to determine whether he would be a hero or a wimp. That day he proved he was neither. He went to school as a sophomore, he ended the day as a murderer.

I heard about George's problem on the news and was surprised when his mother called and asked me to visit him. I never really thought George cared for me all that much, but I agreed, knowing that he had maybe one more shot at getting his life in order.

When I arrived at the jail he was already sitting on the other side of the wire cage separating the inmates from the visitors. The sorrow of a thousand regrets were packed into hollow sockets that once held bright eyes. This frightened, exhausted boy had been the victim of a family situation beyond his control, but his choices had made him a murderer. I felt strange as I stepped into the room, knowing that, at this moment, the spiritual rubber had to meet the road. I didn't want to deal with a problem of this magnitude, but dealing with it meant a possibility of real life for George.

— — Old English had a word that was used regularly in jails and prisons. Every establishment had its own "turnkey"—a keeper of the keys. This was the guy that had the real power in the jail. His physical size didn't matter, his education meant nothing nor did his abilities. What mattered most was that piece of metal he held in his hand. That key he held meant freedom when it was used. When the turnkey passed you by, it meant liberty was another day out of your reach.

I realized that's what I am—a keeper of the keys to kids who are in prison. The Lord has given us a ring of keys to help teens discover their freedom in him. The keys come in different shapes and sizes. All are different expressions of the gospel, a word of encouragement at the right time, a loving rebuke, going to a basketball game, a discipleship class or, in George's case, visiting a jail.

But the key is not effective without a turnkey. The gospel key is no more than lofty words unless someone, a turnkey, takes the key, places it just where the imprisoned one needs it to be, and gives it a turn. At times I'm called to use it in a hostile environment when the imprisoned may not even want freedom. But the opportunity God has given me as a turnkey is an awesome position, a life-giver, a freedom-maker, even when the situation is an ominous one.

As I looked George in the eye that afternoon, I didn't even have to ask. He took one look at me, grabbed the wire cage, and began to cry. "Glenn, help me. I need Jesus." So I took out my keys, and before the meeting was over, he was free. He was in prison but he was free. I was skeptical. I mean, twenty-to-life is a pretty strong motivation to ask for divine help. I wasn't sure if it would last. But a couple years later I received a letter from his sister, whom I later led to Christ at a youth camp. In that letter, she shared how he was still serving the Lord and had begun a Bible study in his cell block.

The greatest thing about being a turnkey is that we have the power to give freedom away to all who want it—even in prison. ♡

The Art of Listening

Samuel's eyes grew heavy with sleep as the last embers of the fire went out in the temple. With shadows from the dying flames dancing on the walls, he lazily drifted between consciousness and sleep. His eyes finally closed in slumber a few yards away from the ark of the covenant, the symbol of God's presence in Israel. As the cool night air drifted through the temple, he was awakened by a voice calling out his name.

"Samuel."

He stumbled out of his bed and sleepily shuffled to his guardian's room. Eli was old and overweight, and had no control over his ne'er-do-well sons, Hophni and Phineas. But he loved Samuel, and since Samuel came to live in the temple, Eli had treated him as a gift from the Lord.

Stopping a moment to listen to the old priest snore, Samuel tiptoed in and awakened the gentle giant, "Here I am, Eli. You called." Eli was mildly annoyed by the intrusion into his dream world and quickly dismissed the boy, telling him to go back to bed. He'd hardly begun to settle in, when Samuel came back saying, "Here I am, you called me." Again he was dismissed, this time with a frustrated edge to the words.

After the third time, however, Eli got the message. God wanted to speak to Samuel.

Eli bent down to look at Samuel face-to-face. Samuel stared into the old prophet's eyes as Eli said: "The next time the voice calls you, Samuel, answer by saying, 'Speak, Lord, for your servant is listening.'" As Samuel went back to his bed, he shook his head, wondering if perhaps it had all been a mistake. Perhaps he *was* dreaming, even now. Just as he had almost convinced himself, the Lord spoke again, and Samuel answered as instructed, "Speak, Lord, for your servant is listening."

The words Eli gave were good advice for Samuel and they're great advice for us.

"Speak, Lord, for your servant is listening."

A genuine voice from God is a rarity these days, and it was no different in Israel during Samuel's boyhood. There was "no open vision" is how the writer of 1 Samuel put it. In a day when God's voice was silenced and Jehovah's memory was relegated to after-dinner talk, God nevertheless opened up dialogue with humanity again through the open ears and tender heart of a young boy. And it's here that Eli showed his wisdom. He probably could have been defensive, "Why isn't God talking to me instead of Samuel?" He could have been lazy, seeking to rid himself of the interruption so he could get back to sleep. But Eli wasn't hurt that God spoke to Samuel. In fact, there seemed to be excitement and anticipation in his voice, and my gut tells me that Eli didn't sleep a wink that night. With a smile he encouraged Samuel to go for it. And a kid learned the art of listening to God.

It's the same conversation I've had with my teens, especially those getting ready to get extreme for Christ. I encourage them to listen and to give their whole heart, and their success is my success, because since I've entered youth ministry, that's what my life has been about—trying to help young ones listen for the voice of God and encouraging them to say, "Speak, Lord, your servant is listening."

There are times I need to heed my own advice. Because there are times I get tired—deeply tired—of the struggle. I struggle with the weariness of wariness, and just as the Father begins to speak, my sleepy spirit doesn't hear or doesn't recognize his voice. I've grown so accustomed to the war, to telling others to listen, I forget that God desires to speak to me, too.

I have to become my own Eli. I have to say, "Glenn, take some time, even if it's just a little, and let the words of Samuel become your herald cry too: 'Speak, Lord, for your servant is listening.' You're good at what you do. You can run a youth program with your eyes closed, but can you master the art of listening to God as he speaks to your soul, speaking words of encouragement for problems and vision for your future? Can you listen to him as he reaffirms your ministry or lovingly rebukes you?

Can you listen as he warns you of danger or sets your mind on that one kid who's stolen your heart?"

Samuel closed his eyes every night in the same place as the ark and I live in the same shadow. But living or working in the house of God can sometimes make anyone jaded. Still, there was a heap of years when God's voice wasn't perceived in Israel— not until one boy heard God speaking to him in his slumber.

The God of Samuel is calling.

"Speak, Lord, for your servant is listening." ♡

A Lesson from Mount Moriah

His heart stopped when he heard the request. Abraham had hardly heard the words when their full impact left him catching his breath. He found himself swallowing the lump in his throat and blinking back stinging tears. After finally receiving the promise of a son from God, after 99 years of praying and waiting and finally holding the promised child in his arms, after seeing Isaac grow and mature, after seeing, knowing, and believing that God keeps his promises—*God now asks this?*

Take Isaac, the promised son, to Mount Moriah. Tie him up. Take a knife. A sacrifice.

But *why?*

We can only imagine Abraham's thoughts as they took the long way to Mount Moriah. Perhaps Abraham was hoping that if he took his time, God would come to his senses and change his mind. But Jehovah was quiet on the journey. Isaac must have sensed the tension as his father nervously avoided eye contact. Tough trip.

Somewhere along the way, though, something happened deep in Abraham's soul. With every minute that the heavens were silent, Abraham's faith battled his fear and in the end, faith won.

As they threw the donkeys into "park" and headed up the hill, he told his servants, "We will worship and then *we* will come back to you." It wasn't cockiness or arrogance, but his words reflected the true hallmark of what made this man different from all others—*he truly believed.* Even if God had to resurrect Isaac from the ashes, Abraham actually believed that he'd be bringing his son back down the mountain alive.

Isaac wasn't stupid, you could hear it in the question, "The wood and fire are here, but where is the lamb?"

The reply? "God will provide the lamb." Though he could have resisted and overpowered his elderly father, Isaac learned how to believe from his dad. In a gesture of profound trust, he offered his hands without resistance.

The last few seconds were frozen forever in Abraham's mind. His raised arm was on the downstroke, sweeping toward Isaac's heart, when it was stopped in mid-air by the strong hand of an angelic being. The words the angel spoke were more than comfort. "Abraham, don't lay a hand on the boy. I know that you fear God, because you have not withheld from me your only son." The words were confirmation of what Abraham had learned long ago. When you can trust God enough to give him all you have and all you are, you are forever convinced that nothing is too hard for him.

It was easy for me to trust God for the impossible when I first met him. After all, when I first experienced new birth in Christ and looked back to the alternative, it was no contest. Jesus granted me a new lease on my life. The daily, abundant life that Christ offered was revolutionary in comparison to the hopelessness that I knew before. I remember believing that God could do anything. I really believed that God actually dealt with the people I prayed for *while I was praying*. I actually believed that when we prayed, God could do the miraculous.

I hadn't learned the cynicism of experience. I hadn't yet learned what so many older brothers and sisters in Christ were experiencing: that as you walk with the Lord, your faith grows calloused and your heart grows hard. I hadn't learned that when you live for Jesus for more than a couple of years, you have a right to doubt God's voice. I hadn't learned the awesome price of having to get back to a place of childlike faith.

That's the journey so many of us are on—wanting to believe God can do anything, but fighting negative example and experience that limit God's power and influence on our lives, until our faith resembles a reed bruised by the lessons of experience and callousness and doubt.

It's apparent that some lessons are better never learned. Thank

God Abraham never learned them. Otherwise he wouldn't have been willing to follow God's voice, and we wouldn't have this incredible example of faith about believing that God can do the impossible in our lives.

I have one opportunity at this life, one opportunity to be used of God to effect a change that will have eternal results. I can't afford to live in the normal way because there's a generation taking their cue from me. If I'm willing to go the distance for God, so will they. If I'm willing to follow God's voice, so will they. And if I can believe that God will do the impossible, they'll be willing to get on the altar as a sacrifice to God's purposes, too.

God wants to do the impossible in my life, not just the everyday, not just the ordinary, not just business as usual, not just as Abraham but also Isaac. He's asking me, like Isaac, to offer my hands to him as an instrument of worship, offering myself as a willing participant in my own divine plan.

There's wood and fire—can I believe God enough to be the sacrifice? ♡

Stretching

Two days of driving down the West Coast, from the high desert of the Yakima Valley to Los Angeles, and we were ready to get off the van. I was taking a group of our students on an inner city missions experience. We were committed to spending a week in an inner city environment, which included sleeping in a flop house and working in various community ministries on Los Angeles' east side. Though I had tried to prepare the teens as best I could, I wasn't quite prepared for reality's cold slap in the face as we pulled up in front of our "home" for the week.

I had a feeling that something was wrong when I heard the sirens and saw the flashing lights of the police cars. (I've always had a keen insight into the obvious.) Fire trucks, a paramedic unit, and an ambulance were all blocking the front door of the hotel.

I was immediately greeted by our guide, a college kid who looked to be about eleven years old.

"Oh, hi! As you can see, we've had a minor little problem here," he says with a nervous chuckle.

"Really?" I said, squelching my own.

"Yeah, some kid was shot in the lobby. It was a gang-related thing. Didn't kill him, they just wanted to scare him." Then he looked back to the teens in the van and said, "Hey, you guys ready for a fun week or what?"

Several wide-eyed girls began to cry.

At that moment my first protective instinct was to turn around and go home. But I was no stranger to the inner city and felt that if we were careful, we'd be okay. As I called the senior pastor for an emergency briefing, I was thankful for the good working relationship we'd cultivated. Ultimately, our conversation pivoted upon one question he asked me: "What's your gut tell you, Glenn?" I responded confidently, "Well, the kids are scared, but I think we'll be okay. This will only make us more careful."

The easy thing would have been to go home, but these overly-protected, middle-income kids needed "stretching." They had never been exposed to the harshness of a culture steeped in despair and I wanted to see them come home different people. But I also had a responsibility to them and their parents, and in the 20 minutes that followed, I went through an agonizing process of trying to decide what to do. There was no right or wrong way. It was a matter of trying to determine what God's voice was saying through the fray.

Stretching is always an uncomfortable experience. In most cases you try to use stretching exercises to your advantage—picking and choosing the times and places where you can push the limits in the life of a kid so they will see Jesus in a different way, so they'll love him more deeply, so they'll respond to him with more dedication. But God always has a deeper agenda than any of us realize. Bank on it. The times that I choose to make sure that kids are stretched are invariably the times when I am stretched as well. In his hand we are all still being formed, still being shaped, still being fashioned into instruments of praise that will draw attention to him so that what people see is not us but Christ in us. I had desired for that to take place in my kids, but God started the week off by stretching and changing me. I determined that we would take on the risks and stick it out.

So the week began with all of us being shocked into the culture, and we truly felt like missionaries. That initial incident set the tone for an amazing, life-changing week. The seven days we spent there were filled with one story after another of adolescent (and adult) metamorphosis. The girls who cried when we first pulled up cried again when we left, only for the exact opposite reason, and I truly came back home with a new crew. Of all the ministry trips we've taken, this trip to Los Angeles has been my favorite, because it was there that I was stretched the most.

God knows how all of us benefit from a good stretch, and chances are the reason we have so many unexpected problems is because we've yet to learn the benefits of submitting to it without complaining, groaning, or wishing we were doing something else.
But like a stretch in the morning before we begin a day's activity, those

times are usually followed by a flurry of activity that results in victories beyond our comprehension. The Bible is full of stories of men and women who show us this. Being stretched means that God is apparently confident in our ability to make it through, becoming more like him in the process.

Are you being stretched? Take a deep breath, chill out, and hang on—the day is just starting and God isn't finished with you or me yet. ♡

Do You Think They Get It?

When my wife shared the news that she would be giving birth to our first child, I had mixed emotions. We had tried for months to get in the family way with no results. So when she told me we were going to have a baby, I was shocked. "How did this happen?" I said. (Duh.) On the one hand I was happy. For days I went around with an incredibly stupid grin on my face. But, oddly enough, I was also frightened—frightened of messing this parenting thing up.

But God has been gracious to us. Though Rhonda and I still approach parenting with a healthy fear of the unknown and a dependence upon God's wisdom to sustain us, for the most part it's been an incredible experience. I'm father to three boys with personalities so different and unique, you'd think they were from different families.

As a youth pastor to my 16-year-old, I sometimes wonder if he's catching all this stuff I share regularly with the rest of the youth group. Any kid in our group knows that the one thing I keep hammering is not just knowing Jesus but living for him in a practical way—sharing him with a world that needs desperately to see believers who are "Jesus with skin on." I know it's becoming an overused expression, but it truly captures what I want them to discover about serving others while serving the Lord. Quite honestly I've wondered if my son is buying all this Jesus-with-skin-on stuff. Is he really catching a vision of living for Jesus, not just in his words but also in his deeds?

If you're a parent as well as youth leader to your kid, you may have the same questions. Let me encourage you with something I found on

The People Who Brought You this Book...

invite you to discover MORE valuable youth ministry resources.

Youth Specialties has three decades of experience working alongside Christian youth workers of just about every denomination and youth-serving organization. We're here to help you, whether you're brand new to youth ministry or a veteran, whether you're a volunteer or a career youth pastor. Each year we serve over 100,000 youth workers worldwide through our training seminars, conventions, magazines, resource products, and internet Web site (www.youthspecialties.com).

For FREE information about ways YS can help your youth ministry, complete and return this card.

Are you: ☐ A paid youth worker   ☐ A volunteer   480001

Name _____

Church/Org. _____

Address   ☐ Church or ☐ Home _____

City _____ State _____ Zip _____

Daytime Phone Number (_____) _____

E-Mail _____

Denomination _____ Average Weekly Church Attendance _____

The People Who Brought You this Book...

invite you to discover MORE valuable youth ministry resources.

Youth Specialties has three decades of experience working alongside Christian youth workers of just about every denomination and youth-serving organization. We're here to help you, whether you're brand new to youth ministry or a veteran, whether you're a volunteer or a career youth pastor. Each year we serve over 100,000 youth workers worldwide through our training seminars, conventions, magazines, resource products, and internet Web site (www.youthspecialties.com).

For FREE information about ways YS can help your youth ministry, complete and return this card.

Are you: ☐ A paid youth worker   ☐ A volunteer   480001

Name _____

Church/Org. _____

Address   ☐ Church or ☐ Home _____

City _____ State _____ Zip _____

Daytime Phone Number (_____) _____

E-Mail _____

Denomination _____ Average Weekly Church Attendance _____

Call toll-free to order:
(800) 776-8008

BUSINESS REPLY MAIL
FIRST-CLASS MAIL   PERMIT 268   HOLMES PA

POSTAGE WILL BE PAID BY ADDRESSEE

YOUTH SPECIALTIES
P.O. BOX 668
HOLMES, PA 19043-0668

Call toll-free to order:
(800) 776-8008

NO POSTAGE
NECESSARY
IF MAILED
IN THE
UNITED STATES

BUSINESS REPLY MAIL
FIRST-CLASS MAIL   PERMIT 268   HOLMES PA

POSTAGE WILL BE PAID BY ADDRESSEE

YOUTH SPECIALTIES
P.O. BOX 668
HOLMES, PA 19043-0668

my computer screen one evening. We had just finished our Wednesday youth service and as I was leaving, I discovered that Jason had typed out his thoughts on my computer. So as you read, imagine that it's your kid doing the writing and let the words motivate you to keep doing what you're doing, because the truth always produces fruit, even in your own child.

A Death that I Can Really Live With

My father just finished delivering one of the most powerful sermons I have ever heard. It was about dying to sin, using Romans 6-8 as the scripture. I had heard it many times before, but had never really got it until tonight. He kept telling us to imagine the pain that Jesus felt on the cross, and to realize that while he was hanging there, he saw us. He saw me. And it was my sin that put him there. I never really grasped it until he read a really old poem by Horatius Bonar:

I see the crowd in Pilate's hall, I marked their wrathful mien
their shouts of "Crucify!" appall, with blasphemy between
And of that shouting multitude I feel that I am one
And in that din of voices rude I recognize my own.
'Twas I that shed the sacred blood, I nailed Him to the tree
I crucified the Christ of God, I joined the mockery
Around the cross the throng I see, mocking the Sufferer's groan
yet still my voice it seems to be, as if I mocked alone.

It was then that I got it: Dying to self and living to God. It is really an amazing concept. It was also incredibly hard for me to understand—but I got it. When I heard that poem, I realized what it meant. He died for me, even though he knew that it was my sin that put him there.

Dad then walked us to a casket in the corner of the room. Inside the casket was not a body, but a mirror. A mirror that would show us what we were before we died to our old self and became new in Christ. After seeing that I couldn't take it anymore. I sat down, put my face in my hands, and cried. No—wept. I mourned for Jesus' death. I tried to visualize the pain that he went through, tried to imagine the wounds and the blood. But all the gory details of the matter were lost as I saw him in my mind's eye. It wasn't his wounds that communicated his pain and finally got through to me. It was his face. Or rather, what I recognized on his face. I saw the agony that he went through, the incredible pain. Then, as the camera of my mind closed in, I saw something within the agony: Love— love for me. So that's why he did it. I got it. And then I saw a tear roll down his face. It was then that I realized that I put him there. I wept, begging forgiveness for my part in his death. And God forgave me. I gave him my sins and I died to them.

I am now dead.

But I am more alive now than I have ever been before.

One thing I'll say about Jason—he's *Jesus with skin on* to me. Thank God he's getting it. ♡

Hold On

Youth ministry had suddenly become
very complicated. After 10 years of working with kids in a church
youth ministry setting, this was too much. I was driving home after
spending two hours at the hospital ministering to a teenage girl. A
suicide attempt. Alicia had a tough life at home but over the several
months she had been involved in our ministry, I felt like we were making
real headway. She had made a confession of faith and, despite almost no
parental support at home, had begun the process of learning more about
Christ and living for him. And now, suicide? I was floored.

When I walked into her hospital room, I suddenly felt very old.
There, in the bed by the window, was a baby. At 14, she'd had more
heartache than most adults have in a lifetime, and at a moment when the
pressure peaked, and Jesus was veiled behind mixed emotions and
confusion, she tried to end her life. Without speaking a word, the painful
expression on my face and my upraised hands asked the question,
"Why?" She answered, "Gosh, Glenn, I don't know." She began to cry. I
sat by her bed and we talked about her making it through. No heavy
counseling. No sermonizing. Just a youth pastor who loved her enough
to come at 2 a.m. and stay there until she went to sleep.

As I drove home, I felt like quitting. I told the Lord, "It was a lot
easier when ministry was just hanging out with kids, God. This is
becoming too heavy." I felt utterly useless and longed for the days when
working for Jesus was simpler, less complicated. I yearned for the days
when I served Jesus out of childlike simplicity. It was then that the Lord
spoke to my aching heart through the tape deck in my car.

As I was driving the deserted streets of Yakima, Washington, I
pushed in a Bob Carlisle tape I had purchased from the Allies concert
we'd just had at our church weeks earlier, and the song "Hold On" filled
my car. Never before were words in a song more appropriate for a
moment. Nestled in those words was a reminder from the Creator of why

I was created, an invitation from the divine to a weary soul. Bob Carlisle's voice echoed the heart of the Father that night, *"He's calling you, he's calling me / Oh can't you see, we can be like children again / …Calling you and me to the family of God."*

As I laid my head down to sleep later that night, the words to that song soothed and sent needed healing to my heart and soul as God dealt with the weightier issues of my life, my calling, my ministry. I remembered that night that my responsibility to God is not to have all the answers to all the problems that teens face. My role is to have a child-like faith that will draw others unto him and give them his words.

I awoke a different man, a Lazarus. I began ministry with a renewed outlook and a new lease on life.

Six years later, I found myself back at square one. A different city, a different youth group, but the same desperate cry from the pit of my being. At 40 years old, I've long since given up on trying to keep up with the teens I'm called to serve, but I love doing youth work, I love kids, and that's always been enough to keep me going. But this February, amid the normal course of ministry, my faith was rocked to the very core. Nothing could have prepared me for that afternoon: My oldest son. A tumor between the muscle and bone of his thigh. Cancer? Wouldn't know for sure until the procedure.

My wife and I walked into Jason's room the night before we traveled to the University of Florida for the surgery, and we watched him as he slept. We stroked his hair and silently remembered: Seeing him the first time as an infant; marvelling at the miracle; wondering what we did to deserve such a wonderful gift. We had faith in Christ, but we were scared, too.

It was then that God sent me another reminder of his care. On the eight-hour trip down to the hospital, Rhonda and Jason were sleeping and I was surfing radio stations looking for something to keep me awake. I was pushing the "seek" button and barely recognised a familiar sound when the channel changed. I quickly flipped the channel back and immediately, the car was filled with the presence of God resounding in the voice of Bob Carlisle—again:

"We must hold on, when there's nothing left to hold to, but the hands of Jesus reaching out to me and you / Hold on, when there's nowhere left to go, for the Father's arms will carry us on through..."

Lazarus was back! My faith was reaffirmed, my soul was strengthened, and I was ready for whatever was to come over the next few days.

The next few days were a blur. Jason was fine. The surgery successful. No cancer. No problem. Whew!

As I write this, I'm in my office 10 months later, looking at the CD cover of an aging rocker with a powerful voice, a powerful faith, and a soul that God has used to help an aging youth pastor over the tough spots in his life. And I'm thankful for faith, for music, for kids, for many more years of seeing God work in my life.

Thanks, Bob. And thanks, God, for using him. ♡

He Must Increase, I Must Decrease

The river was a flurry of activity. Ever since John began his preaching on the banks of the Jordan, a never-ending stream of people made their way to its banks to hear the prophet's words. Many were convinced that John was the messiah and came to repent and be baptized. Others came to hear his words, and still others came to gawk at the crazy holy man, hoping to see him eat a bug or something. A wave of God-consciousness was sweeping Judea, and multitudes were drinking deeply from the well of renewal.

John feared no one. His public rebuke of Herod Antipas for having an adulterous affair with his brother Philip's wife made him no friends with the tetrarch. But John was fast becoming known as one who heard the voice of the Lord. The spotlight gave him a bit more scrutiny than most, and with that scrutiny a small measure of safety. People were repenting, coming back to the God of Abraham through John's message, "Repent and be baptized." So it seemed only fitting that Jesus, too, would go to his famous cousin before he started his public ministry.

We have no record of whether they were friends as children, but knowing the kindred spirit that Mary and Elizabeth had during their pregnancies, chances are they not only played together but were close. I wonder if John ever spoke to Jesus about the urgings in his heart to share God's words? Did they go through bar mitzvah at the same time? Did Jesus ever say to John, "I've got a secret I'm *dying* to share with you?" We'll never know in this life. But one thing's for sure, when the time came, John didn't hesitate to tell the world who Jesus was and what position he should hold in the hearts of men.

Jesus waded through the crowd of spectators and found a place in line. When it was his turn, Jesus stepped forward. The two relatives greeted each other, and in a moment recorded by Matthew that peers into John's spirit, he says, "You want *me* to baptize you? You should be baptizing me." John's awkward discomfort is obvious. "Let it be so for now," Jesus says, "it's important that we fulfill all righteousness." With an attitude of reverence and awe, one cousin baptizes another cousin, one servant baptizes another servant, one sinner baptizes one who would become sin for all.

The Father's voice from heaven thundered his approval and as Jesus walked off, John declares, "Behold the Lamb of God who takes away the sin of the world." At that point, the focus shifted and John's ministry became less and less important.

Succinct and to the point, John let his followers know flat out that the whole purpose for his ministry was to prepare the way for Jesus, his cousin—the son of God. John's words were right on the money. "He must increase but I must decrease." The words were spoken as a fact, but reflected an attitude from the heart.

He must increase but I must decrease.

Though spoken 2,000 years ago, the words are still packed with the secret to happiness and purpose in this life—it's not found in the chasing of dreams and successes but in simply knowing the secret to touching the heart of God.

He must increase...I must decrease.

It seems strange that, in ministry, we should struggle in the arena of self. We, who are supposed to be living examples of the Christ-life, fight with keeping self under control. We live in a religious culture full of big egos and hollow commitments; of unrealistic expectations from those who talk big, but walk small. A genuine voice from God is seen as too extreme, and the message is, many times, hidden by the messenger.

You struggle with it, too. You know what I'm talking about: Times when you were upset or hurt because your idea was turned down. Times when you copped an attitude because others didn't see things your way. Times when your ego was bruised when someone else got the credit for what you did.

Face it, we're fragile—which is precisely why John's message is so important. The only way for you to truly be okay with self is to allow Christ to increase and self to decrease to the point that self just doesn't matter in comparison to Christ anymore. Kids may be impressed with personalities. Sports stars and singers can wow a starry-eyed teen. But the real nuts and bolts of making teens disciples for Christ isn't done by personalities. It's done by people like you. People who give themselves over and over again to kids. People like you who have decreased to the point where the predominant personality in you is not you—it's him.

When egos don't matter anymore, it's okay for one of your volunteer staff members to get the hug rightfully meant for you. When he increases and you decrease, you're motivated more by the results than by the credit. When Jesus increases, you won't have to search for joy in the day-to-day work of ministry; it will be your strength.

John lost his head at Herod's bidding. But the real truth was that John had already been lost to the gospel. His head, his hands, his heart were God's property. It could have been a frightful death, but John died a happy man. Egos don't mean much when you're facing eternity with Jesus as your total source.

John's words are your ticket to joyful ministry.

He must increase...I must decrease. ♡

Surviving When You've Blown It

Gino was his name. The resident eighth grade thug in the Christian school our church operated. Still early in my ministry, I was the junior high school teacher as well as the youth pastor, and it was my job to put junior highers through their educational paces. He was strong-willed, stubborn, and had an attitude bigger than his five-foot-nine-inch frame. Still, I had hopes of reaching Gino before the school year was out.

Gino was a casualty of life and, with him, things were never dull. Invariably, before each day's end, he would say something obscene to a girl, challenge an authority figure, or shake down some poor kid for the tastiest morsels of his lunch. Daily I would seek strength to resist the urge to strangle this creation of God gone amuck.

Each day my assistant would search me out with the latest additions to Gino's rap sheet: No homework, rotten attitude, threats. Constantly deceiving, constantly manipulating, Gino was an unholy terror. Each day my anxiety level increased, and by mid-year I was a basket case. I could actually feel the old-age lines being etched into my face.

Finally one day I snapped. After a smart remark, I called him to the office. For 20 minutes I let him have it. In his face. Three inches from his nose, every ounce of frustration and anger focused at his wide-opened eyes. When I was finished and he was back in his seat, I thought, "There. That'll teach him." I felt better after unloading and was determined to ride him hard until he changed. Every 15 minutes I was back at his desk making sure that he was working hard. "Come on, Gino, step it up." I'm sure that afternoon made the top 10 on his list of worst days.

An hour or so before school let out, on my way back to his desk, I noticed something peculiar. When he sensed that I was coming, the hairs on the back of his neck bristled, and his shoulder muscles tensed up. He knew I was coming and he was preparing himself. I've never considered myself unfair or cruel. But this teen was steeling himself against me, getting ready for the war. *He viewed me as the enemy* and it bothered me—a lot. The mental picture that came to my mind was of a five-year-old hiding under the bed to escape the hand of an abusive parent.

I walked up to him, gave his shoulder a squeeze, and spent the next hour agonizing over the fact that, as someone called to touch kids' lives for Christ, I had failed miserably. The apostle's words to the Ephesians were pounding in my heart *"...Do not exasperate your children."* This day changed my ministry to every teen that followed Gino.

Gino fit no mold. This kid wasn't inspired by me, didn't respond to me, and that's why his lack of progress was such a hard thing to take. Gino evoked a response from me that wasn't Christ-like, a response that made me feel...sinful, out of control. The more I lost it, the less I felt acceptable to God. That day God vividly reminded me that I wasn't acceptable to him because of my great teaching or abilities as a youth pastor but because of the central truth of the cross alone. Jesus died for my sin and made me acceptable to the Father.

Failure is a familiar word to you and to me. It's a part of the gig that we never get used to. We never like to be confronted by our inadequacies. We never like to be reminded that we don't have all the answers, and that sometimes, despite our best planning, we blow it. Yet here's the great secret: While it's never God's will that we fail, God has placed a mechanism into each of our failures that enable us to be more like him *after* each failure than we were before.

In my failure that day, I realized that Gino in all his rebellion wasn't nearly as bad as I was in my authoritative smugness. I presented to him a flawed vessel, and through grace I was restored. It was a pretty humbling experience but it felt like a cold drink of water on a hot day, refreshing and invigorating. If we learn anything from the scriptures about men or women of God it is how they reacted when confronted by their failures. When we blow it, we present ourselves as willing participants to God and he lovingly takes the broken pieces, molding a life that is truly a "new creation."

After a night of soul-searching, I came into our school staff meeting the next morning and asked forgiveness from those who had witnessed my encounter with Gino. It was awkward but necessary, and that morning we all became accountable to each other again, allowing our lives to be open to loving correction. I then called Gino outside on the school steps (I can only imagine what he thought). We drank a Coke together and I asked his forgiveness. It was difficult for him to say, "I forgive you," and we talked for awhile. Though it was only a few minutes, I felt like a lifetime of crud had been washed away.

I was also privileged to witness a change that day in Gino—his shoulders relaxed, his smile appeared, and he actually enjoyed school for awhile. In the years that followed, Gino still had problems, but that singular moment defined our relationship as long as I was his teacher, and it's defined my role as a youth pastor ever since. A humble response saved my relationship with Gino and opened up avenues to care for a hurting family.

How? A week or so after the incident, Gino's mom caught me after school. I almost expected a rebuke but her spirit was appreciative and thankful. Their family, she said, had suffered because of church leaders who were authoritarian but not real, who believed in discipline but not compassion. This incident was one of many that helped rebuild trust and confidence in the body of Christ for them.

What? But I thought I failed!

A failure yielded is a tool in the Father's hands. ♡

A Youth Pastor Lived in Buchenwald

Situated over the main gate, the clock still reads 3:15 p.m. That is the time that the Buchenwald concentration camp was liberated on April 11, 1945.

The 700 children that walked out of the camp that day had one man to thank. Jack Werber was a gaunt little Polish Jew who was stooped over from years of torture. Though he was underweight from the near starvation diet he was placed on, he walked as a giant before the children. You see, Jack Werber was a youth pastor in the truest sense of the word. He was responsible for hiding and, consequently, saving the lives of those who should have been killed.

Jack was sent to Buchenwald in 1939, ripped away from his wife and 14-month-old daughter.

Buchenwald was a work camp for thousands of prisoners, mostly Jews, but also political dissidents and criminals who were incarcerated there before it became a Nazi death camp. Those detained were regularly tortured. Death was an insidious part of life there. Men and women were detained in separate quarters and most of the work was done in the quarry, but there was also a textile mill and other factories where materials for the war were manufactured. Inmates were fed a near starvation diet and every morning the first item of business would be to stack the bodies of those who had not made it through the night.

Because of its size, the Nazis relied on a large number of criminals who were there before the war to run the day-to-day operations of the camp. In most cases, these trustees were more cruel than the Nazis themselves because they feared losing their positions of authority.

In every task given him, Jack Werber performed with diligence and stamina, not wanting the Nazis or the trustees to find a reason to want him dead. A dream drove him on, a dream of one day seeing his wife and daughter again. As the long nights passed, he would long to hold his daughter Emma, to sing songs to her of Jehovah's faithfulness, to hold his wife and be a family once again. For five years he held on, pushed himself, forced himself to do work that no one else would do, because of the power of that dream. Then in 1944, only months before Buchenwald was liberated, the dream was shattered.

In October of 1944, a group of 1700 Jews arrived. New arrivals stayed in a small detainment area made up mostly of tents. As they made their way into the camp, Werber found a friend from his hometown of Radom who was surprised to see him still alive. They were told that Jack Werber had been killed and cremated. His father even bribed a Nazi S.S. officer for Jack's ashes and the family conducted a funeral service for him. The conversation also revealed that Werber's entire family—his mother, father, his sisters, and his wife and baby—had been transported to Aucshwitz, another death camp, and gassed shortly after the funeral. His shoulders sagged as Werber wept openly. All the years of hanging on, of daring to dream of a life the way it used to be, were all gone. For the first time since his detainment, Jack Werber wanted to die.

For days he sluggishly went about his duties. Several times he was almost shot because he did not work as he had before. Werber had lost all hope—that is, until he saw the children.

Of the 1700 Jews that arrived, 700 were children. This proposed a peculiar problem. Those children 10 years old and up could work on the daily work details but those younger than 10 were either transferred, sent to the hospital for experimentation, or summarily executed. The detainment area was filled with children and Werber knew that there was no way they would survive if they stayed there.

So another dream came to life in Jack's mind. His own child was gone but he could see to it that other families did not suffer the same fate.

Werber became an ambassador of deliverance for families he didn't know. Working with the prison underground, he helped get the older ones assigned to light work details. He had other papers forged so that those slightly younger were now 10, and therefore able to be assigned. That left another 600 or so children that simply had to be hidden.

Even though the Nazis had relinqushed most control to trustees, it was still no easy task. Many times they moved two or three times a day. Others could be absorbed into a larger barracks. He began a food drive with those who received smuggled food from the outside. Every detainee was encouraged or forced to give a little of their food so the children could survive. Members of the underground would not report the dead for several days so the bread intended for them would be given to the children. They even started a school for the children to keep their moral high. In the school they learned about their God, and in the middle of hell itself, children were told of God's delivering power.

At Buchenwald's liberation, as the Nazi officers and soldiers being processed looked on, a group of 700 children walked out of the camp led by Jack Werber and those who helped hide the children of Buchenwald.

Lest you miss the parallel, there are similarities that I want you to see:

Jack Werber loved children not his own.
He had a dream for families to be together in God's purpose.
While others gave up, he still believed.
He was a protector from the enemy.
He had to lose his own life to discover his divine purpose.

A youth pastor lived in Buchenwald, and a deliverer lives in you. ♡

When God Changes Your Name

Truman Procopio was the name given me by my parents the day I was born. (Stop laughing.) My first and last names are anything but common. Jokes about Harry S. Truman and Truman Capote, not to mention Pinocchio, were the standard name jokes I dealt with during my boyhood.

In my early orphanage days, I didn't even know I had a middle name and I hated the names I did have. Oh, how I longed for a name that wouldn't evoke a smart remark, a plain name, an ordinary name—a John, a Billy, a Barney or Fred (the Flintstones were big when I was a boy). You can only imagine how excited I was the day I discovered that I not only had a middle name but it was a fairly normal one.

One Christmas my father sent a box of toys to my siblings and me. As my oldest brother Ronnie opened the box, he began distributing presents. The first thing out of the box were beautiful football helmets to the guys, tags attached—Ronnie's first, then Mike's, then Bobby's, then Glenn's. "Hey," I said, "who's Glenn?" With the sage wisdom that only an older brother could muster, Ronnie said, "It's you, stupid. It's your middle name." He had such a way with words. This news was big to a seven-year-old. My response was one of pure joy tempered with just the tiniest bit of unbelief. I didn't want to get my hopes up just in case this was a cruel joke. "You mean, it's me? My middle name is Glenn?"

"Glenn."

I said it over and over again. "Glenn, Glenn, Glenn."

It rolled off the tongue like a poem. It was succinct and yet sophisticated. Ordinary and yet extraordinary. I was reborn. I could deal with anything that life threw at me as a boy because I had a name that wouldn't be insulted.

"Glenn, with two 'n's," I said to no one and everyone. The two "n"s at the end made it sound even more masculine. I stood taller, walked more confidently; even ventured a Clint Eastwood squint as I meandered down the hall that day. Things were never going to be the same. I had a new name and a new lease on life. It's kind of funny when I reflect back upon it. Why I made such a big deal over a name is beyond me, but the confidence that new name gave me was very real.

God has been known to change a name or two also. My favorite story is of Abraham.

When Abraham's name was changed, it was used to affirm the promise God was making to him, from Abram, meaning "father," to Abraham, meaning "father of nations." God chose to use a name that would be a testimony of a work that hadn't yet taken place in Abraham's life. Not only had it not taken place, it seemed downright impossible. To those who didn't know Abraham, it would seem incredibly ironic, at least until Isaac was born. After all, a guy 99 years old with no offspring (at least by his wife) being called the "father of nations?" C'mon. But it was true. God changed his name as a promise of the miracle then fulfilled the promise.

That brings me to a question. Is it remotely possible that God is wanting to change your name, too?

Is there an area of your life that seems impossible to get a handle on? Your thought life? Your consistency? Your critical spirit? Your short temper? There may be a hundred other options. Pick an area in the secret corners of your life that no one else may know about, an area that seems the most impossible for God to change.

If you were in the market for a new name, how would you change it? From "Doubtful" to "Faithful?" From "Lazy" to "Motivated?" From "Insecure" to "Confident?" If so, do something you encourage kids to do: Dare to believe that God can effect that miraculous change in you. Through the brokenness of a humble heart, allow Christ to rule the darkness of your life. Believe that God can indeed change your name and produce the righteousness of his character in you. Then begin using your new name in your prayer time. I'm not just being poetic, I'm being practical. Begin speaking and living as Abraham did, as if the miracle had already taken place, as if God were already on the scene whittling away at your inconsistencies to transform you into a radical believer.

John tells us what we are yet to be is still being scripted by the Master Playwright, who is getting ready to open up the third act on our lives. What you are yet to be is still within the realm of God's possibility, if you will dare believe that he is still writing the finish to your life.

When God changes your name, it's with the desire to change you as well.

So what's in a name? Everything we dream to be. ♡

Zaccheus Speaks

I can't believe today's turn of events. I can't believe how I feel at this moment. Either I'm dreaming or I'm different—definitely different.

I was hoping just to see Jesus, get a glimpse of his face. Had to be inventive. It wasn't my shortness that forced me to climb that tree today. It was the fact that I wasn't wanted anywhere near the crowd. Tax collectors aren't exactly the class of people you show off to a visiting man of God.

So I climbed the tree partly out of curiosity, but partly also because I was tired—tired of being the brunt of everybody's ridicule, tired of leering stares and words spoken behind my back. I was tired of people patronizing me when it was time to pay the taxes and then turning on me when I did my job. I was tired of cheating people, tired of buying friends, tired of being isolated. Mostly, I was tired of being lonely.

I didn't really think anything was going to happen, I just wanted to be a part of something big. And I heard that this Jesus was *big*. So I climbed a tree, just wanting to see the prophet. I didn't want him to pray for me or recognize me or anything. I simply wanted a glance at him. I wanted to see what a man of God is supposed to look like. I wanted to see if he was different from the leaders in our town.

What I didn't know was that Jesus wanted to see me, too.

I was motivated by loneliness and curiosity but guess what motivated Jesus? Love—for *me*. Can you believe that? I had never met him and I wanted to see him. He wanted to see me, too—but from the inside out. When he called my name, I didn't have to climb down. I fell down, gasping:

"You want to eat at *my* house?"

As I walked next to Jesus down the road to my door, I felt every eye on me, but I didn't care. All that mattered was that for the first time in my life since my father died, I met someone who wasn't ashamed to be seen with me or my friends. And who, more than that, seemed to care.

We rolled out the red carpet for Jesus and his disciples. The religious leaders waited outside the door, and Jesus spent the evening in my home. We ate and drank together. We talked and laughed, and I listened. He spoke words of life, words of peace and hope. He spoke of a kingdom that will never end in our future and a joyful life for the present.

As I looked into his eyes, they sparkled with a knowledge of my life. Though he never said a word, he knew me—nothing was hidden from him. He didn't make me feel guilty, he made me feel comfortable, and I knew that I could never be the same again.

I'm ready. Ready for a new life, ready for a new reason to get up everyday, ready to experience the joyful life Jesus spoke about tonight. I have no idea what I'm going to do for a living. Who ever heard of an honest tax collector?

It's funny, though. I can't stop smiling. I'm making a list—and I'm trying to imagine what the people on it are going to think when I pay them back. How can I tell them what has just happened in my life? Jesus has made a small guy suddenly feel very big.

Thanks, Jesus. I may be short but, because of you, I can now touch the face of God. ♡

192-10

God goes to amazing lengths to get his message across to me. Case in point: When we developed a prayer pager ministry with our kids, I thought it was kind of a nifty way to allow them to know that, at anytime of the day, they could get a prayer request through to me. Not only was it a cool idea, but through this little pager, God has taught me a lesson in gratitude that could never ever be found in a seminary textbook.

Each teen was assigned an I.D. number. Furthermore, I assigned one and two digit prayer request codes for the different types of requests that a teen might have: *1* was personal sickness, *2* was school problems, and so on. So when they had a request, they'd simply call the pager and enter their I.D. number, the "#" key, and finally their prayer request number. The number *10* was "I'm praying for you, Glenn." Frankly, I didn't expect that one to get much use.

The first couple of weeks we had it going, I received pages pretty regularly but as the novelty of it wore off, I would receive a page only when kids were really in need. For the most part, the pages consisted of anything from school stress to broken relationships—with one exception. For months and months after we started the prayer pager, I received the same page everyday, and everyday I was humbled by the message the page represented.

The page was this: *192-10*. It was Garrett. He was praying for me. Again. And again. Every day.

Garrett is a very special kid. He has blond hair, sparkling eyes, a vibrant faith, and muscular dystrophy. When we first met, he was in the early stages of the disease and you would've been hard-pressed to know that there was anything wrong with him at all. But over the course of the last couple years, the disease has progressed to the point that he gets around mostly with the aid of a wheelchair. It doesn't stop him, though. His heart still burns with a passion for Christ that other kids have a hard time understanding. Garrett has experienced a richness with God that goes way beyond how he feels at the moment.

He wakes up with his body in pain, and he deals with it all day until he goes to sleep at night. The only respite he receives is when he is sleeping, except for those nights when he wakes up crying out in agony. Garrett knows that there is more to serving Jesus than feeling good, more important things.

Of all the kids I know, he is the one you'd think would have a major problem with God. Yet when you see him pray, when you watch his expression and listen to the words, there is a unusual holiness about it all. These are not bitter prayers. They are the cry of a heart who wants desperately to be used of the Lord—a heart-wrenching expression of a soul longing for a deeper touch from Christ and a way to flesh out his experience so his world will be impacted because of his life.

That's why every page I receive from him is such a humbling experience. Here's a kid who is hurting and yet he's praying for me. *He* takes *my* name before the Father. What an honor. What it must be like in heaven when his prayers reach the throne of God! "Shh, everybody! Gabriel, put down the horn—it's Garrett!" Here's a kid who fights battles of doubt, who has more than once wondered about Jesus' mercy. And yet, every time he does he has come to the same conclusion: "Where else am I going to go? Serving Jesus is worth it." He knows that one day he will walk—either here on earth as a result of God's healing power or on streets of gold in heaven. And knowing that's enough for Garrett.

Everytime I receive another *192* (It's Garrett)—*10* ("I'm praying for you, Glenn"), I'm immediately humbled that a teenager who complains so little would care enough to pray for an adult youth leader who knows his own tendency to complain a lot, even if privately. Each time I see that page—*192-10*—I'm reminded that my problems and stresses are minor in comparison to this kid whose body is racked with pain while his heart knows the cutting edge of God's grace.

A month or so ago, Garrett called me. The teen years are tough enough when you're healthy, but when you've got muscular dystrophy, the variables are much more intense. He's growing up, thinking about his future, about girls, about going to the prom. The stuff other kids take for granted are major hurdles for him. He was confused and hurting, and he called me. Never have I been more aware of the importance of the words I shared than when I was on the phone to this angel unaware. We talked about faith and purpose, about the will of God, but in the end I was pointing him back to the one he already knew so well. I gave him some practical advice but I pointed him to Christ. I pointed him to Christ, just as he had done for me through his many pages.

192-10.

You have never met Garrett but you know someone like him. God cares for you deeply. And he's placed loving reminders of his care all around you—in a letter or a smile, or in the hug you get from a teen passing in the hall. It might even be in the toilet paper on your front lawn.

Or it might be in the irritating, loving "beep" of a prayer pager paging—*192-10.* ♡

Torture

Only after four days and three nights of continuous torture did the North Vietnamese soldiers bring Jeremiah Denton into a sterile, brightly-lit room. Television cameras were poised awaiting the show. They had been preparing Denton for an interview with a Japanese newsman known for his sympathy to the North Vietnamese cause.

In 1966, the Vietnam war was at its peak, and POWs—prisoners of war—were worth their weight in political bargaining power. The North Vietnamese were wanting to make an example of Denton, forcing him to denounce his government and win the sympathy of the eastern world. But heroes are a rare breed and they overestimated the affect of their torture techniques on this determined pilot.

They "prepared" Denton by starving him and subjecting him to a standard technique they called the "ropes and iron bars." The prisoner's arms were pulled behind him and tied together at the elbows. His wrists were then locked in "torture cuffs" and "jumbo irons" were placed over his ankles. A thick iron bar was slid through the "jumbo irons." The torturers then looped a rope around the bar, over the shoulders, and pulled the prisoner's head between his knees. For four days and three nights, Denton was subjected to this treatment and wasn't allowed to go to sleep.

As the cameras moved in for a close-up, he was expected to make a statement condemning the United States' war effort. Denton, slumped in a chair, rolled his eyes wildly, staring at the ceiling. He began to systematically blink his eyelids as he was questioned. The blinking eyes gave Denton the appearance of a man who had lost his senses. Then, surrounded by his torturers and their cameras, Denton gave this statement: "Whatever the position of my government is, I believe in it, yes sir. I am a member of that government and it is my job to support it and I will as long as I live." The attention of the North Vietnamese shifted to the interviewer. Amazingly, the only one in the room that understood English was the interviewer. "What did he say?" they asked. "Was it damaging to the North Vietnamese cause?" The interviewer, obviously impressed with Denton's resistance and loyalty, told them the statement was unimportant and managed to get the tape out of the country.

As the tape was aired, a keen telecommunications expert picked up on Denton's eyes. The blinking was a message. In Morse code Denton spelled out the word *torture*. Later, the North Vietnamese, after discovering what Denton had done to them, brutalized him over and over. The news of his torture drew international attention to the plight of the POW.

Amazing creativity. Amazing resolve. A prisoner of war risked the tenuous life on which he was holding to bring attention to the fact that he and his comrades were being tortured by a merciless enemy. The only opportunity he had of enlightening the world was the faint hope that someone would pick up on the subtle message he was leaving them— blinking eyes that spelled out a horrific one-word message.

Warfare with the enemy over the lives of young souls is sadly similar. Walking the streets of our cities and the hallways of our schools are the POWs of the war with Satan. Their gaunt souls and confused philosophies give dreadful testimony to the enemy's hatred of God's creation.

Because there is so much that is expected of youth leaders, oftentimes we find ourselves occupied with the "busyness" of ministry. We're so consumed with "doing" that we forget to be "seeing" as well. We forget to look into the eyes of the kid we're talking to—to see if, in the midst of a conversation, their eyes may be sending us a message of the same sort of spiritual torture.

One night after our youth church service, I was helping Justin put the drums away. Justin was a talented 14-year-old who was just beginning his adolescent growth spurt. He was still short but his feet were big and his voice was changing. His family was changing, too. His mom's first marriage ended in a painful divorce and now she and his step-dad were having difficulties that I was unaware of. Up to this point, I hadn't seen any indication of the problem from Justin. I say "hadn't seen" because in all honesty, it was a busy time of year, my guard was down, and I really don't think I was observant enough. But simmering beneath the boy's quick smile was a kid who was hurting from the memory of the past and the uncertainty of the future. Here was a POW who needed to know that God still cared for him.

As we joked and laughed while putting the drums away, something strange happened. I wish I could think of a specific "thing" that caused me to gaze in Justin's soul that night, but I can't. I just remember turning to thank him for the help, to say "goodbye," "see ya next week"—something. However, instead, I put both my hands on his shoulders, looked into his eyes, and I saw it—the rhythmic blinking of a soul sending a message of "torture" to someone who was looking for it and would care.

"Justin," I said, "I believe in you."

The words didn't matter. The love was what he recognised. He buried his head in my chest and began to weep. I was a little surprised. The other staff turned around and, like a family, we huddled around him and loved him out of the POW camp he was in. This is why I got into youth ministry, and it's times like these that are the reasons I stay. Programs and ministries, events and trips, they're all cool. But what makes our choice to serve kids worthwhile are times when God opens our spiritual eyes revealing the hidden message, the torture a kid is facing.

If we're not careful, we will miss those hidden messages altogether. ♡

Spit, Sight, and Appreciation

John 9

"ALMS! ALMS! Come on people, how's a blind man supposed to make a living if you don't chip in? Hey, thanks a lot, Mister, I appreciate it!" (*Cheapskate.*) "Hey. What's all the fuss? I *know* you're not trying to push me off this corner. Stop crowding! What's going on? Who? Jesus? The prophet? He's bringing a lot of people with him. Time to bring out the big guns: *ALMS for a poor, miserable blind man! ALMS!*

"What? Who are *you*?! Disciple or not, if you're going to stop here, you at least ought to drop something in the cup. What's that? Who you calling a sinner, chump? If I could see, I'd wear you out. Who's that? Jesus? He's talking about me? 'It was neither that this man sinned or his parents.' Yeah! You tell him, Jesus! High five! Oh, sorry, lady.

"Hey, wait now. What's that spitting and squishin' sound? Oh, it's *you*, Jesus? Well, no sweat, just keep doin' what you're doin' I'll keep collecting. Wait! What are you doin'? Whoa—gross. Now, I know you didn't just put that spit-mud on my eyes. That was mean, Jesus. I would have never thought you'd do something like that. I can only imagine how stupid I look right now. You want me to go where? The pool of Siloam? Do you know how far that is?! Yes, I'll wait and I'll listen. Yes, I understand. In order for God's power to be displayed—yadda yadda yadda. Great. Thanks a lot. Bye."

Man, I hate it when prophets come to town. They all have their different angle, and when they leave, the crowd is whooped up, I'm still blind, and they don't even drop a coin into the cup. But they say this guy's different. They say he really does heal. I don't guess I got anything to lose. But Siloam?

Walk. Walk. Walk. Man, I'm gonna need a new pair of sandals.

"Yeah, thanks a lot, Mister. Right, I got it. Five more paces ahead. Yeah, I know there's mud in my eyes. Thanks a lot, bucko. *See* you later, too." *Everybody's a comedian.*

"Okay, this is it. Jesus, wherever you are, I hope I'm not in for another disappointment. Brrr, the water's cold. Yikes! The clay's stuck to my eyelashes. Here goes. Time to open up. Come on...come on...Oh, oh—am I imagining it? Do I see light? L-l-light?! It's coming into focus. *I can see! I can see!*

"Hey, Mister! Wait! Look! I'm *seeing* you later! I am! I used to be blind, but now I can see! What's that? What am I going to do now? Forget Disneyland! I'm going to find Jesus and see *him*. Oh, how I'm going to see *him!*"

We, too, are blind you know, still regaining our sight as our vision of him becomes increasingly clear. Daily the colors get clearer, the image becomes sharper, and the reality of his relationship becomes more wondrous. Seeing Jesus had to be a worship experience for any blind man he healed. How to thank God for our sight? Thank him like a blind man. All we have to do is turn our new eyes behind us and see *them*. They stand there, needing help, needing hope, needing—sight. If ever there were a time we wondered how we could thank God for *our* sight, we need look no further. ♡

"Whose Kids Are These, Anyway?"

There's only one way to describe my youngest son Jared. He's a sweetie-pie. Not a masculine way to describe him, and when he's a teenager he'll probably thrash me when he discovers this description.

But that's what he is. Jared Procopio is made of the same stuff as ginger snaps. He has a genuine sweetness toward other people, with just enough spice to make him all boy, and an innocence that is refreshing in a home filled with ministry stresses, school schedules, and financial worries. Whenever we're arguing—that is, discussing with passion—who does what and when, Jared will come up with a great line or a comment that helps us remember that we have a pretty terrific family, that we've got a lot to be thankful for, and that the same God who has taken care of us thus far is still watching over our home.

Recently we were on a ministry trip with our students, and Jared picked up a pretty nasty fever that skyrocketed quickly. By this time in our parenting journey, Rhonda was an old pro at handling temperatures, but this one even made her nervous. I was at the sessions with the teens, leaving Rhonda by herself with the little guy. She contemplated taking him to the doctor but he began to respond to the regular medicine. So she prayed and put him to bed. I came in late, and Rhonda brought me up to speed on how he was doing. As she went back to sleep, The Question came playing back in my mind.

The Question first came 15 years ago when our firstborn Jason had his initial minor health problem. It was a fever during the hottest part of the summer during a week of youth camp. Rhonda and I both overreacted, and as I was walking across the campground to get the van, I prayed the prayer of a young father freaking out. "Help, God! Don't let him die!" I know it sounds silly but I was genuinely afraid we might lose him. It was then that The Question was posed for the first time.

The Holy Spirit asked, "Hey, Glenn, whose kid *is* this anyway?"

I responded to the Lord in an honest prayer that was as sincere as it was desperate: "God, you have blessed me and Rhonda with this child to raise into a decent human being, one that will love you. He's our child, God."

God's next words were a prompting from a Father wanting to teach his son the true secret to fatherhood: "That's true, Glenn. But do you remember? Nine days after he was born? You gave him back."

I did remember. Jason's dedication. With an entire chapel full of friends, we dedicated him to God, just as Hannah had given her son Samuel to God's service in the Old Testament. I swallowed hard and in an act of soulful submission every bit as determined as Abraham's, I surrendered Jason to God again. I drove to the hospital that day knowing that our future, his future, truly belonged to the Lord.

The Question came again when Jeremy, our second son, was born. Six weeks after his birth, we were told during a routine examination to take him immediately to the cardiac care unit of Beaumont hospital in Detroit. They had found a congenital heart defect, a hole between the chambers of his heart. We raced to the hospital and there we wrestled with God. The same fear as with Jason, the same anxiety, the same questions, the same answer, the same result. Six years after the problem was found, he was given a clean bill of health without ever having surgery.

Both of those experiences were on my mind the night of Jared's temperature scare. While I was listening to Jared sleep, I realized something wonderful. As Rhonda and I have tried to raise our children, God has been raising us. As we have tried to fill their lives with the certainty of a love that would never end, he has been filling us with the same. As we've tried to reflect delight in their successes, he has rejoiced in ours. As we sought to share their pain and cry with them when they were hurting, God was hurting with us.

It was then that I truly understood what God was doing, and I was humbled by the thought. By posing The Question to us in different situations with each of our boys, God was showering the full impact of his love on my children, through Rhonda and me. His love wasn't filtered through a parent's ego or a vicarious dream, but because he brought us to the point where we believed they were truly his children, he could love them completely through us.

It may have been our hands, but it was his touch.

It may have been our words, but it was his comfort.

It may have been our tears, but it was his peace.

It applies to parenthood—and it applies to our ministry with kids.

As you endeavor to draw young people to Christ, he's drawing you close as well. Your choice to give your life for youth is his design to make you more like him. If God is to truly love kids through you, then you have to answer The Question, too.

"Whose kids are these anyway?" There can be only one answer.

If you're frustrated with your ministry, chances are God's asking you The Question.

If you're fearful of rejection, chances are God's asking you The Question.

If you've never been confronted by the possibility that God has placed you in youth ministry to change you as much as he changes kids, then I know God's asking you The Question.

It may be your advice, but it's his character being shared.

It may be your heart that's broken, but it's his pain.

It may be your vision, but it's his plan.

"Whose kids are these, anyway?"

They're his and he's loving them, really loving them through you. ♡

A Father to the Fatherless

Couple of weeks ago, I was observing the wrap-up of our weekly youth church service. It had been a good night of making a difference in the world. By allowing God to change one part of their lives, they had taken the first step to changing their world. The Holy Spirit blessed the words. The kids bought the vision. And I was watching our volunteer staff help these hungry, enthusiastic teens process what they were feeling in their hearts and decide how to put flesh to their feelings when they went to school tomorrow.

Off to one side, Shane was talking to one of our junior highers. I don't exactly know what Shane was saying to him, but I've come to trust Shane's wisdom.

Rewind 14 years earlier—Detroit, Michigan.

I was working in a small church in Detroit as youth pastor, music leader, and schoolteacher. Shane was one of my students. As a teenager, Shane demonstrated a remarkable hunger for God and an excited desire to be used of the Lord. He was a really great kid, despite his home. He had a mother who daily walked before her kids with a Christlikeness seldom seen today. However, Rodney, Shane's father, was an alcoholic, so life in the Taylor household was a constant walk on eggshells.

One Sunday evening Shane's dad came in. When the altar call was given, Rodney went forward. He had been drinking, and while everyone was delighted about seeing Rodney finally make a profession, Shane stayed back. He wouldn't go forward. He loved his dad but wasn't about to lay his heart on the line again. Well-meaning people at the church came up to him after the service, saying, "Aren't you excited, Shane?" He responded politely but inwardly a conflict seethed.

The next day, knowing that Shane didn't believe any lasting change would occur, I stopped by his desk during school. I wanted to encourage Shane. Maybe this time *was* different, I said—although I didn't really believe it either. I knelt down by his desk and said, "You're not buying it, huh?" When he turned to talk to me, I saw a single tear well up in his eye and then roll down his face. "You know, Glenn. He does this every once in a while. He'll come in, make this big show, get everybody's hopes up, and in the end it never lasts. I want to believe, but I just don't think it's gonna happen."

What do you say to a kid who's in that kind of turmoil? What can you say? You point them to the Lord. We broke out the Bible, and in a singular verse that I used over and over in numerous conversations with him while I was in Detroit, God gave Shane a hook to hang his faith on.

Here it is, Psalm 68:5a—more of a title than anything else: *"A father to the fatherless..."* Shane's father had abdicated his responsibility to the bottle and God's promise to Shane was that he'd fill that void. And those were words that Shane bought, big time.

Sixteen years later, through circumstances far too complicated to explain, he and his wife Marilyn, who was also in that first youth group, live in the same city as I do and they are joyfully serving as volunteer youth leaders to my present group. (Boy, do I feel old.) And whenever Marilyn or Shane talks to a kid, I have an emotional flashback.

Sixteen years of maturing hasn't dimmed Shane's love for Christ and his desire to be used of the Lord. Marilyn and he are teachers and, as such, they have a true ministry to their students and also to kids in our church. Whenever Shane shares words about Christ, they are invariably seasoned with his tears as he talks about the God who truly became a father to the fatherless. God has given me a weekly reminder that, at least for one hurting kid, I had a hand in changing the world, because now they are changing the world too, one kid at a time. ♡

Hidden Worlds

"*There is nothing...hidden that will not be made known*," Matthew wrote in his Gospel (10:26). I thought of this verse that evening after our last session. The previous two hours had dripped with emotion as well as information, and because of what had transpired, our group had walked away profoundly changed.

We had spent two days in the mountains of the Pacific Northwest on a prayer retreat. Over twenty kids and staff had looked forward to this last session with anxious anticipation. After two days of talking to God and searching their hearts through various exercises, I felt the teens were starting to be totally honest with themselves and with God about their inner lives. I had a feeling that we were going to be pleasantly surprised at what would happen at the session, and I wasn't disappointed.

Before our last activity I'd given the teens a piece of string and a piece of paper. The emphasis of this particular prayer retreat was "Barrier Breaking," an attempt for teens to take careful stock of their spiritual condition and then allow God to break through the barriers they'd discovered or uncovered. After writing their particular barrier on the paper, the kids were to fashion a cross with two sticks they would find and tie the paper to it. The crosses were then to be brought into the last session.

It was fascinating watching them come in with their handmade crosses. The crosses they'd made reflected their own particular personalities. The jocks went for the big and bad, the meek and timid chose smaller sticks, the creative ones came in with interesting variations to the assignment. But all were ready. You could read it in their faces— young souls who had taken a journey. And as they entered the room, it was surprisingly quiet, almost solemn, indicating the emotional turns in the road they'd traveled.

Two unique individuals were part of our group. One was Josh. About a year earlier Josh, a kid with attention deficit disorder, had been living on the streets of Seattle. His drug problem had forced him out of his house and he'd bounced from one group home to another. He'd stumbled into our group after finding Christ through a street ministry. Part of their help to him was to send him to a treatment center in Yakima and we were the fortunate recipients of this angel with ADD.

Though intensely in love with Christ and delivered from the addiction that once controlled his body and soul, Josh was a unique individual to say the least. At age 18 he still had to be watched over like a junior higher because he was spiritually illiterate and constantly fighting the battles of his former culture. More than one time in our youth group meetings during an intense moment of spiritual discovery, Josh's lack of respect and strange sense of humor sent the entire group rolling on the floor, blowing the whole point I was trying to make.

But there was also a sensitive side to Josh that made all the negative qualities palatable. Because he had received an abundance of love, he knew how to freely give it.

Alek was another player in this drama. His slurred speech and slow gait made him a target for many of the others who didn't know his story, a story that was about to be revealed in glorious fashion.

With these two characters added to the mix, the stage was set for God to do something awesome.

As we were gathered together in a circle, the teens were asked to share what it was they tied to the cross—being as general or specific as they wanted to be. The circle started with Josh and he shared how he had to resolve his bitterness with past pains. His statement set the tone for teens who followed to share similar scenarios—the need for God to break the barriers of internal scars left over from their hidden worlds.

Teen after teen shared and the theme was consistent: Pain. Pain. Pain. By the third kid's response, I noticed that Josh was acting peculiar. He was sitting on the seat back of his chair with his arms folded across his chest and his eyes closed, and he had begun to rock back and forth on his seat. With every testimony shared, the rocking became more pronounced until soft whimpers escaped his lips. I was getting a little concerned. The air was heavy with the emotion of kids experiencing the pain of their peers. It was a moment when God's heart was beating in the lives of his own. And yet Josh's rocking and whimpering began to increase. C'mon, Josh, I thought, hang in there. Don't freak on me. We only had a few more testimonies, the last being Alek.

As Alek began his testimony, Josh was listening intently, his closed eyes and taut face communicating more than a thousand words. Alek began speaking in his broken, slow voice. "Most of you know me... I've...gone to this church...for the last few years. I know most of you...are wondering why I...walk slow and...don't speak as fast as some of you." Every eye was on him, every ear tuned to his words, while Josh kept rocking, his hands across his chest and his eyes closed yet still absorbing the power of the moment. "Well," Alek went on, "my paper spoke of pain...too. 'Cause when I was little...my parents got a divorce...and they had a big fight...over who got to keep my brother and me.

"Well...my mom won, and my Dad was mad. So one night...he just showed up...drunk...picked me up and threw me into the back of his car. Well...he had an accident...and I was thrown...through the wind-shield and hit my head pretty hard." Josh was rocking quickly now, the chair moving. "And I have always hated...him...for that. And that's...why I talk the way...I do and walk...the way I do. I need to forgive my Dad."

Silence.

Then Josh stopped rocking and bolted out of the room, screaming. Through the window I saw him run to the volleyball court and wrap himself around the steel pole. The screams were unintelligible, agonizing expressions that came from deep within his soul.

A millisecond later the room emptied out and the entire group had joined Josh. Each of these young souls became entangled in a massive embrace, each voice echoing the painful cries from hearts that hurt, one for another. The cries from their souls were targeted at the enemy but they reverberated the message each one needed to hear at that moment—someone actually did *feel their pain.*

The brutal honesty of the moment enveloped my heart. Through the obedience of one kid who was in tune with the Father's heart, the entire group was able to process and release the pain that had accumulated until that moment. God used Josh's painful experiences so that he might be able to truly relate to the pain of others. Indeed, his pain made him more sensitive to God.

Pain is part of the territory of youth ministry. The kids you encounter may come from different homes and families but a thread of pain runs through most of their houses. All teens have their own particular story and hidden world of pain they keep shielded from the eyes of others. Part of helping kids discover Christ is helping them let him deal with their pain.

While it's never easy hearing the struggles of kids, it's comforting to know that when they hurt, the Father hurts with them—often through the heart of another believer who's tuned in. That day I learned something from a kid who didn't know theology or the ins and outs of the Bible, but he knew how to let God love others through him. And when you love with the heart of God, then the Father helps you see with spiritual eyes.

God lets you see their hidden worlds. ♡

Reflections in the Wall

We were there as sightseers, a family in Washington D.C. for the day, taking in the sights—the Smithsonian, the Washington Monument, the whole bit. The summer of 1983 was a time of memory-making. Last on our "to-see" list was the Vietnam Veteran's Memorial. Trying to instill a sense of love and loyalty toward one's country in a small boy would not be an easy task, but I was determined to try. I doubted if Jason, three years old at the time, would even remember. But I wanted to give him a memory that would help him appreciate the ones to whom America said goodbye in the Vietnam War.

I wanted him to receive a memory—but I was the one who walked away with a clear image I would never, ever forget.

Although I was a kid during the Vietnam War, I remember seeing the television news footage and often felt a sense of loss when the television camera would show another body draped in a field blanket. The images brought home the stark reality that during times of war, there are casualties, and this one had more than its fair share.

I'd had an older friend who died in the war, and I wanted to look up his name and find it there. The wall is an incredible display. It's called "the wall that heals" because many who have struggled with the anger and grief of losing someone in the war have been strangely comforted by seeing the names carved in the dark stone slabs.

So there we were at the wall, my wife, my son, and I. As we looked for the name, I began to notice those around me. These were the forgotten victims of the war, the people whose lives were altered by a telegram or a knock on the door that ushered their hearts into a world of sorrow and pain.

To my left was a teenager, a girl. On her face was a steely-eyed expression that marked her as one who struggled bitterly. Here was a kid who had lost a dad or someone very close, and the pain of that reality was in her tear-filled, hardened eyes. Her shoulders were tensed, her hands balled into a fist, and she was holding a piece of wadded paper. As my imagination filled in the blanks, my mind kept rolling one thought over and over: "This just isn't fair."

Just beyond her was a woman and two boys, between nine and eleven years old. She stood and stared, and cried. The older son stood reverently at her side while the younger boy, obviously bored, fidgeted. Her red nose and constant flow of tears were a window to the pain of a family caught in the heartbreak of loss, a family desperately trying to find peace after losing the cohesive element of their family. I was tempted to try and say something comforting but no words of comfort came to my mind. Instead, I felt an aching pit in my stomach, and a new sentence formed in my mind: "How can I show them what you were like?"

Lastly, to my right was a group of Vietnam vets. The larger part of the group kept their distance. It's an interesting phenomenon that I'd read about somewhere. Some vets find it difficult to approach the wall, knowing the names of many friends are there. Their repressed anger causes them a great deal of anguish as they fight with the traumatic results of the only war America didn't win. The ability to step up to the wall is an act of healing for some, and the majority of these hurting men seemed not to be ready to say goodbye to their friends or their feelings.

There was one, however, who had no problem stepping up to the monument. In fact, a confident peace resonated through his quiet sniffles as he made a rubbing of the name of his fallen friend. As he held the paper up to the name and scribbled a pencil over it, I was comforted. The tears, though painful, were also full of hope, a hope I couldn't understand—until I saw something. Among the other medals and patches decorating his loose-fitting green army jacket was a pin of a dove. It was easy to fill in the blanks after that. His half-smile's radiance of divine peace made me all but hear what he must have been saying to his dead friend: "I'll see you someday—and this time, no war."

I stood there looking back at the wall, staring at the name of my own friend, reliving the unwritten stories of these three other lives forever changed by a war, and I noticed something else. The smoothly polished stone of the wall showed more than just the chiseled name—it showed my reflection as well. I stared into my own eyes that day and suddenly my heart's cry became crystal clear.

Kids today live in a war zone. Their minds are constantly bombarded with the confusing philosophies of self-indulgence and the lack of values, their friendships are barraged with the need for acceptance and validation no matter what the cost. Even their faith is challenged by the concept of a life with no higher purpose. And into the midst of these walking wounded, God has placed me. And you. Kind of awesome when you think about it, huh?

As you survey your own group's haggard panorama of pain, look at your reflection as well. Stare into your soul as you rethink why you do what you do. If you love kids, you'll come to the same conclusion I did that day. As you are daily confronted with the war-zone needs of the teens you touch, look at your reflection in the wall and be encouraged that God has given you a gift—kids who need you. It's why you are here, you know. It's why you ache. It's why you suffer when a young one under your scope of influence suffers. You've been given the privilege to really love kids and when you love them, you fill in the blanks when it comes to their pain. You don't necessarily look for the details, but you look for opportunities to answer the questions that torment their souls.

The missing pieces of each person's story that day are also strangely relevant to our ministry as well.

"This just isn't fair!"
Life *isn't* fair. That's why we need Jesus.

"How can I show them what you were really like?"
They will know what the Father is like by seeing you and me.

And if, in the midst of it all, they ever wonder, you can assure them that Christ, with a peaceful half-smile, is saying this very moment: "I'll see you again someday—and this time, no war." ♡

Sailing on Ships That Will Never Return

Acts 27:7-13

Paul gripped the handrails tightly as the ship set sail. The wind was calm and the breeze felt good on his face as the small craft headed toward the open sea. Thus far, the trip had been uneventful for the group of prisoners headed for the courts of Rome to stand trial. Among the prisoners, mostly thieves and political dissidents, Paul was somewhat of a peculiarity. Most prisoners on board would do anything to avoid standing trial before Caesar, but Paul was looking forward to it. It was his right to be heard before Caesar as a Roman citizen, a fact that had saved his neck from certain death at the hands of an unruly mob months before.

But there was another reason Paul was looking forward to being heard by Caesar. And that reason was the gospel. Since the day of his arrest, Paul had stood before Festus the Proconsul and even Herod Agrippa, proclaiming the truth of who Jesus was and why this Jew, who was crucified years earlier, was the most important person who had ever lived. Although Paul was heading for Rome, his heart beat for heaven. This reckless love for Jesus Christ drove him on with a desire to share the message with the most powerful man in the then-known world.

On the journey to Rome, Paul had been shown favor by the soldier guarding him. The guard let him greet friends on one of the stops, and it was an evening steeped in memories of Paul's journey to his knowledge of who Jesus of Nazareth was. Remembrances good and bad. Victories won and lost. A night of thanksgiving to God who had been the common thread through it all. When the evening was over, his friends bid him well and spoke of seeing him again. But there was a finality in his words, a goodbye that said much more.

As the ship set out to sea, Paul looked around at the quaint seaport of Fair Havens. It was really nothing more than a tiny blip of a port where people stopped on their way to somewhere else. The thought of spending the entire winter there, though, hadn't appealed to the captain and crew, so they were going to hug near the shore to miss the bad weather and make it to Phoenix, which was more their kind of town.

But Paul knew better. The Lord had spoken to Paul about the trip they would take. Paul knew the ship wouldn't make it and, at that time, he wasn't so sure who would. Paul warned the centurion. But the centurion disregarded Paul and relied on the seasoned sailing pros who saw nothing to fear. So Paul took one last look at the safety of the little harbor, knowing he was sailing on a ship that would never return.

We are, too, you know. When we are born, the ships of our lives begin a journey designed by God himself and, like a vessel that is headed from point "a" to point "b," our lives never pass the same place at the same time ever again. The particular circumstances of our lives happen only once. *Once.* Therefore it is profoundly important that not even a moment is wasted. Psalms 90 says *"...teach us to number our days that we might apply our hearts unto wisdom."*

Good advice. Wise advice, especially to those in ministry. The thing is, when we were spinning our dreams about touching the world for Christ, no one ever told us about the storms we would encounter while sailing on this ocean of need.

No one told us—

- that sometimes our hearts would cry out for understanding.
- that sometimes we would be grateful for one day of rest.
- that sometimes we'd hunger for a word of encouragement or sympathy.
- that our family would bear the brunt of our ministry burden.
- that a burden for a kid could hurt so much.

- that our own kids could grow up so quickly.
- that feelings of unworthiness don't ever really go away.

And when encountering these storms, it's easy to become inwardly focused. Doing so is probably not a bad idea at that point, because when storms do come we need to look inside our souls and see why we are reacting to *this* storm in *this* way.

But we should not make the mistake of letting the fear of the storm stop us from being used. Remember, we are sailing on ships that will never return. The opportunities of today come only today and, despite the world's philosophy, there are no second takes in life. We have one shot at it. Our decisions today will affect ourselves and others tomorrow.

So when the storm is raging, we do what we must, taking care of the important things, our families, our ministries. But we should never forget that the storms are part of the process and shipwreck is part of the miracle of God's sustaining power. There is a lesson to be learned from letting the storm do the work of unsettling us until we realize that, like Paul, the hand of God has never left us.

Listen to his words at the end of this story:

"Men, you should have taken my advice...but now I urge you to keep up your courage, because not one of you will be lost; only the ship will be destroyed. Last night, an angel of the God whose I am and whom I serve stood beside me and said, 'Do not be afraid, Paul. You must stand trial before Caesar; and God has graciously given you the lives of all who sail with you'..."

With every storm we face, an angel is in the shadows awaiting his cue to step up with a message of hope and encouragement. And even if the ship breaks apart, there's a plank with your name and my name on it ready to carry us to safety. For the sake of a generation who needs to see the practical reality of faith in action, we can't waste a moment of time wallowing in self-pity's depressing mire. Too much is at stake. Because we are faithfully sailing on ships that will never return, the ones we touch today may be the ones pulling survivors from the sea tomorrow. ♡

The Legacy

I *n the presence of God and of Christ Jesus,*
who will judge the living and the dead, and in view of his appearing
and his kingdom, I give you this charge.

Preach the Word: be prepared in season and out of season; correct,
rebuke and encourage—with great patience and careful instruction. For
the time will come when men will not put up with sound doctrine.
Instead, to suit their own desires, they will gather around them a great
number of teachers, to say what their itching ears want to hear. They will
turn their ears away from the truth and turn aside to myths. But you, keep
your head in all situations, endure hardship, do the work of an evangelist;
discharge all the duties of your ministry. For I am ready to be poured out
like a drink offering, and the time has come for my departure. I have
fought the good fight, I have finished the race, I have kept the faith. Now
there is in store for me, the crown of righteousness, which the Lord, the
righteous judge will award to me on that day—and not only to me, but also
to all who have longed for his appearing.

Do your best to come to me quickly, for Demas, because he loved
this world, has deserted me and has gone… Only Luke is with me. Get Mark
and bring him with you, because he is helpful to me in my ministry… When
you come, bring the cloak that I left with Carpus at Troas, and my scrolls,
especially the parchments.

You hear it? It's the sound of a book being closed. The last few
grains of sand in the hour glass slipping through the funnel. The sound of
a ship being towed into the harbor one last time. It's the sound of a legacy
being passed to the next generation. It's a symphony of voices from the
past and present, of victories won and agonies triumphed over. It's the
message of a thousand lessons learned, lessons of instruction and joy, of

righteous anger and love for others, of pain and yearning, collected over decades of ministry—all gathered in a few words written to a kid who was there when it first started.

Timothy was Paul's protégé. Timothy was Paul's "youth group." While Paul wrestled with a call to bring the Christ story to Gentiles, God slipped a ruddy-faced reminder of the need under Paul's nose. Timothy's family were some of Paul's first converts and, as such, they held a special place in his heart—especially Timothy.

Timothy was an eager student, anxious to learn, anxious to please, anxious to capture that "something" in Paul that made him so different from others. That eagerness endeared him to this pioneer of the faith. As Paul touched others, Timothy listened and watched, soaking in every detail, learning from his mentor. Eventually Timothy himself followed in Paul's footsteps and became a young pastor, sharing the source of life that had so radically changed him. You can hear Paul's concern in his first letter to Timothy— sage advice on how to deal with a wide range of problems from stomach ailments to widows and elders.

It was important to Paul that Timothy succeed.

That's why his final words written to the young pastor are so powerful. They paint a picture of care and concern that are lasting. The words artistically craft an image of what a youth leader looks like from the inside out. Interest in little things, gestures of love that are reciprocated, transparency not fearful of being truly shared, and a selfless devotion to seeing the potential of another realized.

One can only imagine the emotion of the moment when Timothy read the letter. Initially the focus would be on practical matters: Get ahold of Mark. Bring the cloak. Make travel arrangements. Get the scrolls together, the parchments, too. But on the journey to Paul's side, the letter would be read and reread over and over again. The central truths would be ingested and remembered and when the time came, the wise words would be remembered and the principles recalled to make decisions.

The three capsules of wisdom that Paul gives Timothy are doorways of success for you and me, too—at least our perception of success. Paul would have been considered a failure and a lunatic by today's standards, I suppose. His words, though, to Timothy are the stuff that legacies are made of.

Be prepared, for tough times are ahead.

Be wise and endure hardship.

Be willing to keep the faith.

Are you surprised? Nothing too profound there, huh? Truth is, that if all Paul had given Timothy were words of advice, the words would have gone in one ear and out the other, but Timothy had seen the words fleshed out in Paul's lifestyle.

Timothy had seen Paul *prepare* for difficulties every time they came into a town. He'd seen him steel himself against religious leaders who were perverting the truth of God's law. He'd picked up Paul's battered body after being beaten and stoned.

He'd read the *wisdom* Paul poured into his letters to the churches he loved so devotedly. The words were like a soothing balm to the hurting in Phillipi, and a scalpel to those cancers growing in the church in Galatia. In all his letters, the words communicated a perseverance to keep going and growing in Christ through *hardship*.

He'd witnessed the determination to *be true to the faith* that had delivered him from the chains of religiosity, a determination that would press him past the limits of human endurance. That's why he could say *"...having done all to stand, stand therefore..."*

And that's the point that brings me to the crux of my matter. What legacy are you leaving the kids in your group? The kids in your home? The words you say will be empty and meaningless, like so much scented fluff, if they aren't backed up by the life that you live.

As you read these words, think of the kids you may have offended without healing, think of the times when, in the throes of a busy schedule, you didn't keep a commitment to your own children, and ask yourself, "What legacy am I leaving?"

Paul was not perfect by a long shot, but his relational legacy is illustrated one more time in these last words to Timothy.

Remember Mark? In the early days, Mark, a young convert,

impulsive and over-eager, had made a commitment to accompany Paul on one of his journeys. When persecution came, however, Mark headed for the highlands, and Paul was reticent to take him again the next time. But here at the close of his life, he calls for Mark.

"Only Luke is with me. Get Mark and bring him with you, because he is helpful to me in my ministry."

It was Paul's way of saying "I'm proud of you, Mark. You've done well." Another disciple is born, another legacy passed on. Paul left the early church in the hands of two young men who had learned the value of walking in the footsteps of a man of God.

There are those walking in your footsteps as well. Look behind you, you'll see a line of future warriors of the faith, and you cannot afford to ever forget it. They will be watching to see if the word you speak so effortlessly is the life that you live in reality.

One day they will inherit your legacy. ♡

Destiny

Moses had seen more of life's extremes at age 40 than he cared to remember. Rescued from a basket in the bullrushes, he'd been raised a son of Pharaoh with all the perks. Prepared for the throne. In a position to change the face of history. But one impulsive act of anger left a soldier dead, the body hidden in the Egyptian sand, and Moses running for his life.

This prince of Egypt, once destined for kingship, was now a terrified fugitive with no prospects for the future. Intimidated by the power of Pharaoh, naive, and forced into retirement before he ever had a job, Moses ran to the desert to hide, to escape his troubles, and to be left alone.

Forty years later, Moses found life in the desert good to him. He found a wife and acceptance into her family. Happiness came easy as a simple herdsman, and for a while he was content to live and die as a shepherd, husband, and father. Though he was groomed for kingship, life's hard blows had left him satisfied with simple survival, hiding from his destiny.

That was, of course, until he saw the bush. Over the years, as a shepherd, he had seen hundreds of blazing bushes, caused from careless fires or maybe lightning, but this was something else—something strange. So Moses decided to check this one out. For someone trying to hide, this was a big mistake. As Moses approached this strange bush that was burning but wasn't destroyed, he heard the voice of God for the first time.

I can only imagine what Moses thought after he came to—something along the lines of: "I shoulda stayed in the tent." In a whirlwind of power and a supernatural voice, God revealed his plan for Moses to deliver Israel from bondage.

Moses' response was much like ours when we come face-to-face with a calling we don't want. He made excuses: "What if they won't believe me? What if they *do* believe me? What if they want to know your name?" What if—? What if, what if. Finally, Moses cast his last and best argument: "God, I'm not a speaker, so please send someone else." In patient understanding, God named Aaron as Moses' mouthpiece and Moses sheepishly accepted.

This is a side of Moses we can all identify with. All of us have been in situations where we've had an opportunity to represent the Lord and blew it. The truth is, it's easier to make excuses and get forgiveness than it is to step out and risk rejection. We've learned to avoid standing *out* for God too much so we're never put in the situation of standing *up* for him. Fortunately for Moses, he learned through God's faithfulness that the reward for obedience always outweighs any risk we take.

This shepherd-turned-servant left the desert as a reluctant recipient of a divine call, a frightened herdsman called to lead God's people out of bondage. But months later, he returned as a reconstructed man of God with four million people following him.

The parallels between you and Moses may seem hidden, but sifting through and finding them is well worth the effort. From the moment you called him Lord, you also made yourself available to him as a servant. A generation of young people are needing a deliverer, and while you may never climb a mountain and pull off your sneakers before a burning bush, the call is no less divine. But here's another thread in this parallel: God may also have to do some internal work on you in order for his purpose to be completed, just like he did with Moses.

Moses argued with God over his ability (or the perceived lack of it). But I wonder how much of his struggle had to do with the ghosts of the past? How much of Moses' reluctance was related to a skeleton in the sands of Egypt? How much of his aversion to stepping out of the desert was that he had to admit he was a murderer?

The ghosts of the past are powerful weapons. And the enemy knows how to use them to limit our effectiveness, robbing us of our creativity, plummeting our self-esteem. During such battles we can't imagine getting through the day, let alone arising above it. Ghosts of the past come from every angle, and they never play fair, attacking when our resistance is down and we are ripe for temptation. But in every season of woe, there is a miracle of reconstruction awaiting to be accomplished—with every ghost of the past, a promise of greatness.

Open your spiritual eyes. You may be surrounded by ghosts of the past and failures of the present, but there is a burning bush calling your name somewhere, and you need only look to find it. Somewhere there are captives that need to be led to freedom and there is a God that is depending upon you to do it. Moses isn't really that different from us, you know. He saw the divine, he was confronted by the need, and he responded to the call.

The divine burning began in you the first time God opened your heart by grace, the need was made clear to you when you made eye contact with that first kid who needed you, and your response to the call has taken you captive. Don't let ghosts from the past diminish a divine future.

The promised land of God's nearness is waiting on you. Don't hide from your destiny. ♡

Runaways

As an eight-year-old who didn't care for life in the orphanage, I often thought of running away, and so did my brothers. We even talked about it. But when you live with nuns who looked like they were too tough for the Soviet women's swim team, discretion seemed to always be the better part of valor. I mean, the thought of having to deal with a nun who interrupted her weight lifting to deal with a runaway pretty much kept us in check. However, after one particularly bad day, our fear was outweighed by our frustration, and my younger brother and I decided to give it a shot.

St. Mary's orphanage was surrounded by fields that were filled with hay, cows, and organic land mines. None of us kids had ever been past the field and had no idea what was on the other side. This particular night my younger brother Bobby and I would go where no orphan we knew had gone before. It was late and dark and the only light came from a small flashlight that wavered with every step that my skinny little legs made.

As we reached the fence, we both felt a roar of jubilation course through our bodies—or fear, I got the two confused as a kid. Past the barbed wire of the cattle fence was freedom. Once we hit the interstate highway, we would hitch a ride with a kind stranger who instantly would be a friend; our hero who would somehow know exactly where we needed to go, who would take us in and help us to get jobs with the circus or the demolition derby or the—okay, you get the picture.

All we needed to do was get past the fence.

Because it was dark, we couldn't really tell what was on the other side and, to be quite honest, we were so excited that we didn't really pay much attention. We didn't realize that eight inches past this particular portion of fence there was a drop-off that led to a creekbed worn away by years of erosion. As I held the wire for Bobby, I was thinking of myself as a protector to my kid brother: "Ah, yes, Robert, you shall grow up to be quite the man. You shall do well and true and honorably. You shall work your way through life and shall be an example of manliness and—AYYYYYYYY!"

I fell off the edge.

Thankfully, my hand managed to latch hold of the barbed wire. Not so thankfully, one particular barb lodged in the lower joint of my thumb. To make matters worse, the soft ground around my feet had collapsed with my struggling, leaving me dangling from that one barb. Bobby began to panic, but managed to calm down after he realized that I was still alive and, as the oldest, would bear the most responsibility. As I dangled, we tried every possible way of pulling me up but the ground was collapsing more and more. Finally we came to the conclusion that we had but two options. Bobby could continue without me and I would sacrifice my life for his future (I mention this option because as a child I had a noble streak, and I knew that Bobby had to go to the bathroom and was afraid to go in a strange restroom alone). Or, Bobby would have to go back to the orphanage, wake up the habit-wearing body builders (for you Protestants, *habit* is what nun's clothes are called), and come to my rescue.

I knew that Bobby would choose option number two. (Did I mention that he had to go?)

As he said goodbye and made his way back carrying the flashlight, I was left hanging there with my thoughts. The sensation was not altogether unpleasant when my arm finally went numb. As I listened to the sounds of nature, waiting, shivering, all alone, I suddenly became aware that the orphanage wasn't such a bad place after all. The unpleasantness was swallowed by the reality that there was a bed that was mine, a roof over my head, and to some degree, safety from danger (if you considered the nuns an occupational hazard).

I lost my appetite for working in the circus, and before too long my ears were treated to the sound that every runaway loves to hear—the sound of your brother being smacked on the back of the head by a nun who makes the ground tremble when she walks. A tear of joy came to my eye when her voice pierced the night (she'd stepped on one of those organic land mines). I thought, *There's no place like home, there's no place like home*, and tried unsuccessfully to click my heels together.

That's when my mouth resounded with my cheer of exceeding joy: "HELP!"

Runaways are a part of the territory in youth work. If you've been working with teens for any length of time, you've received the phone call or had a conversation with a parent who's looking for their kid.

But what about the runaways who never leave home? What about those who for one reason or another have run away from relationship with God? Relationship with parents? Responsibility? A sense of duty? What about those who have run away from the morality or the faith that their parents have painstakingly pumped into them over the years?

In our world of self-centered ambitions, self-centered philosophy, and self-centered theology, our kids are taught that it's easier to run away from problems, especially internal ones, than it is to face them and discover a workable solution. In trying to make their lives better, we've tried to make them easier. But easier is not better, not when it comes to dealing with the inside stuff of relationship and faith and character. Society has left a generation dangling precariously over an abyss of hopelessness, waiting for someone with the good sense to direct their feet to solid ground. That's where you come in. (You knew this was coming.)

Some runaways can sometimes give you the impression that they have no use for you, that they couldn't care less what you think. That you are the biggest dweeb to ever hit the planet. They don't like you and, for the most part, they tolerate your presence as just another piece of furniture that occupies this particular room in their lives. But don't you believe it. Keep hammering away with love, keep encouraging, keep affirming. (Besides, we all know how cool you *really* are.) Now, rest assured, there will be land mines on the way, and you may find yourself the recipient of an undeserved attack or unwanted abuse, but hang in there. One day you'll hear their cries for help, and whether it's you or another youth leader who God uses, you will know that the time, effort, and love you showed that runaway acted like a beacon to bring them back home.

We're getting ready to leave for our fall retreat and, as I write, I am silently praying for a kid who decided at the last minute to go. He's making a big deal about saying he's going so he can look out for his brother, but I know what happened. He's been belligerent ever since he started coming to our church. He makes no apology for the fact that he thinks Christianity is worthless. But this Sunday I saw the facade crack. He was having lunch with a couple of kids from the youth group who have desired to be true light to him. As I sat with them in the mall over french fries, telling stupid jokes and being my dweeby youth pastor self (in a very cool way, however), I saw the lines soften and I knew that this runaway was about to come home. I'm not a betting man, but I've seen it time after time. He's homesick.

And when you're homesick, there's no place like home. ♡

I Feel Like a Used Pair of Shoes

"**F**air-weather eyes" are eyes that are shielded by celebration. You have fair-weather eyes when you see a celebration, but not the need or hurt inside.

On a recent trip to an amusement park with our group, I learned a pretty cool lesson on perspective. I had spent most of the day with my son and a few of his friends. Now that Jason's a teenager, we can enjoy the stuff that he was always too little to do before. We hit every roller coaster, even the one called the "sky coaster." After the fun rides, I decided to do some more slow stuff with my youngest son Jared. We hit the kiddyland and then decided to take the overhead tram to the other end of the park for a bite to eat. Rhonda and I gave him some special attention as we all looked down upon the park from a dizzying height.

The scene was definitely a festival. As I looked from above, thousands walked by underneath, eating corndogs, laughing, enjoying the day. Screams of delighted terror filled the air. And then I saw something else. I saw one of our youth group kids. She was sitting down beneath the shade of a tree, alone. We have a pretty strict rule on these trips. You always have to stay with somebody—nobody is to be by themselves. I kept watching, and before the ride was over, I saw her friends rejoin her. Apparently she had been waiting on them.

As we left the tram, I felt a seed of a thought pop into my mind, and on the bus trip back home, the seed began to grow. I thought about how many times our weekly youth group ministry was similar to that experience. With the active nature of youth ministry, especially in a crowded room full of lots of stuff going on, loud music, and a constant influx of programming, I wondered how many times a kid who was looking for a place to find love and acceptance was surrounded by humanity but left totally alone.

We are confronted by a collage of faces each week. With the new faces coming and going, it becomes more and more difficult to spot the kid who is drowning amid the activity of the celebration. Like the smiling faces in a carnival, detecting the frightened look of loneliness and need in the shadows behind the fun is hard.

Recently I spoke with the parent of one of our kids. The conversation left me with a precise mental image of one of these overlooked "shadow-dwellers." Andrew was having a heart-to-heart talk with his mom about his spiritual journey. Things weren't going so well in school, and he was having difficulty fending off temptation from a variety of sources. On top of that, he felt lost in our group. He came pretty regularly, but he was agonizing and nobody knew or acted like they cared. In words that were as poetic as they were sad, he stated, "Mom, I feel like a used pair of shoes." He felt walked on and used up trying to hang with a faith he couldn't get a handle on. And no one noticed.

I missed it, too. Amid the celebration and festival atmosphere of our weekly service, one of our own was lurking in the dark shade of self-doubt, searching for encouragement to keep going, seeking a reason to celebrate, and I missed it. That familiar feeling of regret visited me and I battled the "what if's" of lost opportunities I'd had to communicate with him the peace of God, the power of God.

All youth ministers have a desire for their groups to grow. In the early days, quite admittedly, my shallow thinking equated success in ministry with how much growth occurred in our weekly meetings. The bigger crowds seemed to validate my existence as a youth pastor. When the crowds were down, my emotions went into a tailspin and I considered myself unworthy of breathing God's air, let alone leading a youth ministry. Thankfully after a number of years, I'm secure enough in my relationship with Christ to realize that my sense of success comes from simply being obedient to Jesus, allowing him to produce the results he desires.

But such a knowledge doesn't absolve me of the responsibility to be truly observant when the ministry does grow, either. While regarding and participating in the joyous experiences of growth, we must take the time to carefully peer into the shadows. For there are those overlooked souls who feel like so much shoe leather, used and abused by this life while trying to hold on to the last shred of their faith.

When I heard what his mom told me, I called Andrew. He was pretty forgiving, if embarrassed that his mom told me what he said. But then we talked about why he felt the way he did, and we tried to somehow make sense of it. I wanted to give him the answers he needed, but during times when your faith is being tested and you are dwelling in the shadows, cute answers are a lousy substitute for a loving heart and the visible presence of somebody who truly cares. And that does not come with one visit.

So, for the future, I begged the Lord to burn Andrew's words into my memory: "I feel like a used pair of shoes."

I use the same words to issue you a challenge this week. Tell your kids of Andrew's story, tell them of a kid who was in the room yet wasn't really there. Tell them the story of a kid who was drowning in a crowded pool.

Then ask how many of them, like Andrew, feel like a "used pair of shoes," too. Look in their eyes, hear their stories. You may be surprised.

Then beg the Lord to burn their faces in your memory.

Oh God, somehow, someway, help me to be ever looking into the shadows, seeking out those who aren't obvious, looking into the eyes of my kids so that I won't miss a thing. Help me to see that which is paled by the celebration. Let me never forget the words of a kid who felt like a used pair of shoes and consecrate me to the task of making sure that no other in my care will never say the same without experiencing your loving touch through me. Amen. ♡

Turf Wars

Facing each other in a room thick with emotion, two rivals sat on opposite sides of the table. And although separated by only 36 inches, the two were worlds apart. All participants were painfully aware that one would walk away the victor and the other would go home beaten and battered, with the woeful realization they had been bested. Steely eyes locked and the silence was finally, decidedly broken.

"I have nothing against you Pentecostals, but we have to have someone else to lead the worship at our rally or I just can't support it. What if some of them start rolling on the floor or something?" With that the meeting was over, and another opportunity for unifying a community was thwarted. You could hear the sounds of "high-fives" coming from the regions of the netherworld.

You know, for a group of people who are supposed to be filled with the love of God, we are so territorial. I've seen "spirit-filled" believers look down their spiritual noses at others who "haven't received" as being slightly more spiritually gifted than an offering plate. Back and forth we go, and it's no wonder that our kids are sick to death of it.

I have a friend in the faith named John who is on the opposite end of the spiritual spectrum from me, but we both share a passion to touch young lives for Jesus. During my time in Yakima, there was a real need for an outreach to help divorced kids. As John and I spoke with other youth leaders in various churches in the city, God favored us. The network thing worked, and youth ministries from all over the city cooperated in pulling it off. During a joint prayer time for its success, as John and I shared, *one* of us was very vocal, and it sounded like this...

"Guys, this is incredible, we are working together, and in two weeks we'll have the opportunity to really meet a need in our community, to see kids who have been damaged by divorce find practical help in dealing with it. But as we begin to pray I have to tell you, I'm a bit nervous. I pray *silently*, and when I'm around others who pray out loud, I am truly distracted. Plus I don't know how I'll react if someone starts speaking in tongues. I don't want to put a damper on this, but is there some way we can come to an agreement to get the best of both worlds?"

In a spirit of cooperation, we achieved a unity of the faith, while preserving our diversity. I didn't tell you whether it was John or me, because some will try to size me up and determine which side of the line I'm on. Therein is my point.

God allowed denominations because he saw that there was a wide diversity of personalities and human needs. Each of us responds to the Lord out of the uniqueness of our particular background. Sizing up a person's denomination will not tell you the size of their heart, nor will it tell you of their sincerity before God or their love for kingdom work. You'll not understand the depth of their commitment or know their tears in the night by denominational tags.

But you'll see the size of their heart in a lunch room or a restaurant when they are surrounded by teens. You'll know their love for the kingdom when they talk about their needy ones. You'll know the depth of their commitment when you see them in a courtroom, being there for one of their own who's gone astray.

All around us there is an army of young people who *want* to join hands and change their world, but they become discouraged because they know how their youth pastor will react if they suggest that we link up with another (especially *that* church).

Shame on us for being so territorial that we stifle the work of God and sell our kids the impression that we're right and everyone else is wrong.

In a stretch of woods in North Dakota, a young boy wandered from his parents' cabin while playing in the snow one morning. As the parents frantically looked for him, snow began to fall. Soon dozens of their neighbors joined in the search, then dozens more, but all came up empty-handed. After an entire night of searching, hope was ebbing away. They knew the boy was in this one area but were unable to find him. Finally, one volunteer suggested to link arms and comb the area in a solid line. A short time after joining arms, they found the boy curled up frozen—dead.

Tears. Sobs of anguish. Then a statement:

"If only we had joined arms before."

Your kids are wanting to make a real impact, they are wanting to link arms with others of different denominations and different churches to effect a change in their world. They'll do it with us, they'll do it without us, or they won't do it at all because their thinking has been poisoned. Look around. There are plenty of unconverted kids in your area, more than enough to fill every church youth group to overflowing.

Hundreds are already past the age of being affected by the influence of your group.

"If only we had linked arms before."

Reach out. Together, changing the world is possible. ♡

Moved by the Word

Nehemiah 8

Out of the ruins. After 146 years,
Jerusalem was a fortified city again. When Babylon reduced the city
of Jerusalem to rubble, all hope of Israel ever rising again was lost.
But this was a new day. Hope arose with the sun as the first morning rays
peeked over the new city walls. Through the leadership of Ezra and
Nehemiah, Jerusalem was safely ensconced. Though lackluster compared
to its former greatness, Israel had a place on which to hang their hearts
again. God's people were slowly rising from the ashes.

As the city rose, there was a need for their faith to rise as well. So
instead of announcing a week of rest after a difficult job done quickly,
Nehemiah assembled the people and then turned to Ezra the priest as
Ezra began reading God's Word.

The crowd was silent, the only sound coming from crowing
roosters and baying donkeys. As squinted eyes filtered the early light, all
focused upon the image of the priest who 13 years earlier began the
process of rebuilding, starting with the temple. Ezra's wooden podium
was elevated so that all could see him. Some fifty thousand assembled
that day. The emotion of the moment mirrored in the faces of the
company. Through a hammering heart and tearful eyes, Ezra opened the
book. As a slight breeze stirred the scroll, a greater stir was taking place in
the hearts of the people.

As he read from sun up to midday, something unexpectedly
marvelous happened. It began with a few sniffles, then sobs, then a wave
of repentance swept over the people. As they heard the heart of God
echoed through his law, the people were moved. For seven days they
listened and were broken. They remembered, and their collective pride
was crushed. They absorbed, and they were motivated to change their

priorities.

God's people—moved by God's words.

This is the way it was intended. God speaks. We hear. We react. We are changed, and then we respond to the newness that the Word has produced in us.

I hear this story and I remember incidents just like that in my life—times when God became real to me by hearing him speak through his Word. Pretense and presumption were stripped away in the knowledge that there is nothing hidden from him. I've known hours when God dealt with my sin through printed words on a page that were alive with his power, moments when repentance was a logical result of humanity being in the presence of the holy. The words of God, reflecting the heart of God, producing the image of God—in me.

I can't help but wonder why we, the "called," find it so easy to neglect the words of the one who called us. We desire to do his will, we agonize over *not* doing it, and yet we don't take time to get his direction and insight to fulfill the task that he asks us to do. We human beings are a strange lot—so demanding and yet so ungrateful, so needy and yet so forgetful, in need of such light but too often content to dwell in the shadows.

A story regarding Augustine was making the rounds through the Bible school I attended. I've tried to validate it and wasn't able to, but it makes for a cool story, anyway. Call it fiction if you want but listen to the point. During the time he was researching his doctrine of illumination, Augustine had a profound experience. He proposed that as we read the scriptures, the Holy Spirit enables us to understand them on a spiritual level that transcends the natural intellectual processes and engrafts the message of God into our hearts. Legend has it that one day his journal entry contained one single word written in print bold enough and large enough to consume the entire page:

"*FIRE*"

Does that ring a bell? Does it bring to mind to moment when God became *that* real to you? Does it evoke an early memory of when just you and God met heart-to-heart over the pages in God's written words?

"FIRE"

Knowing we are safely within the walls of the salvation of Christ, and yet, needy, we open the Bible where God's words reflect the heart of God and we compare it to our own. We are made aware of our own sinfulness and how far we are from what God desires us to be. We repent, casting ourselves before him in humility and tears, submitting to the will of the one who made us his own. It would be worth it if all we did was that, but there's more, something wondrous.

Read Nehemiah again.

After they had grieved before God. After repentance. After brokeness. Nehemiah steps up to the podium, smiling. "Stop grieving now," he tell them. "God has restored. It's time to dance, to feast, to sing. It's time to celebrate." After they had processed the pain of repentance, it was time to rest in the joy of celebration. Celebrating a restored relationship with God and a clearer direction and vision for the future.

When was the last time God's words crushed you? Long forgotten are the days when they would strip away the shallowness of your faith. Long forgotten are the times when in humility and holy desperation you, like Jacob, wrestled with God so that you could be touched by his presence in your life.

Maybe you're going through a process of repentance right now, your heart tormented over the lack of godliness within you. Your sleepless cries going up before the throne of God in genuine sorrowful repentance. For you, it may be time to hear the command that Nehemiah gave the children of Israel that day: "Stop grieving. It's time to celebrate." It may be your time to dry your eyes and look into his. What you'll see is not a look of condemnation or a "you-better-not-do-this-again" frown. What you'll see with spirit eyes is wide-open arms and a smile that says: "Welcome home."

What we are all about as believers boils down to our faith in words that are printed in a book that we call divine. The more time we spend in the book, letting the words press us and mold us, then the more we'll be able to truly reflect the author of the book, who just so happens to be the author of our faith as well.

Oh, by the way, your kids are reading the book, too. They are reading the one written with ink on paper, but they are also reading the one that is being printed through your life. If it is to work in them, it must first work in you.

Open the book. ♡

Staff Confessions

At the 1997 regional Special Olympics in Chattanooga, the crowd had gathered at the McAllie School, some to compete, others to watch and support. The magic of Special Olympics is seeing people—athletes, each with different challenges, striving to be champions and achieving that goal on a scale most of the crowd will never truly understand.

One race in particular captured the essence of the games. As the race began and the runners started their strides, onlookers wouldn't have thought much of it. The times would break no world record, and the face of the winner would never be on a Wheaties box. But the crowd was to learn a lesson about the human spirit that day.

Three runners had pulled ahead and down the home stretch it became clear to everyone that these three would certainly win. The leader of the pack was beaming. His stride was confident, his smile communicating the pride he felt at the moment. As he was peering over his shoulder for one last look at the rest of the runners, time began to slow down and, as if in slow motion, he watched as his competitor, running second, fell and hit the track hard.

Before I share the rest of the story, let me ask a question that might make this narrative a bit more memorable. Have you ever met a "Do-it-all?" You know who I'm talking about. The guy who thinks that no one can do anything as well as he can. Rather than asking for help, he just does the task without using those that God has surrounded him with? The girl who is doing so much all by herself that she is in a constant state of burnout? The guy who wouldn't ask for help in the first place? Well, I must confess to you, that guy was me.

I used to think that my reluctance to give tasks away was due to the fact that I am a perfectionist, especially when it comes to artistic and creative stuff, but that wasn't my problem. My problem was rooted in pride. I had a problem when someone else got credit for something that I could have completed. There was something threatening about someone else getting the attention for a job well done or an activity that went off without a hitch.

Quite a confession, huh? I read the words myself and can't believe how sick my walk with God was back then. Puts a lump in my throat when I think about it. It's taken years, but I'm finally learning the delicate and important art of delegating in a proper spirit.

Thankfully, through experience, trial and error, and the patience of others who saw the calling in me and decided that I was worth salvaging, those days are gone forever. But it wasn't an easy road. Often I frustrated those God had placed around me. They wanted to be used and I didn't—wouldn't—use them. Consequently, I was always frazzled, and there were constant holes in my ministry because I was busy trying to plug every leak myself. I couldn't keep volunteers and, suddenly, on my own, the task of reaching kids seemed insurmountable.

We are all made up of the sum total of our experiences, saint and sinner alike. Though we may be redeemed by a Saviour working to make us over into his image, there is still a mountain of dirt that God needs to move in some of us. And the tools he uses most in his landscaping is *other people.* As he uses others to change you, he uses you to change them. God's will is a circular work benefiting his saints on both sides of any given situation.

Others make our own lives complete. Whether we're talking about a family or a job, a college education or the fulfilling of a dream, our lives depend upon the intricate personalities and quirks of the "others" in our lives. We can't exist without them nor can we effectively touch the lives of kids without them.

Each of us has been given a certain amount of giftedness. Acknowledging that is not a sign of arrogance. Indeed, recognizing the gifts that God has placed in our lives should make us thankful for his love and care. One may acknowledge that she is a speaker, another that he has a gift for music or art, and another a certain flair for counseling. Yet another might have the ability to think through and plan an entire activity and never miss a detail. But even if one person had all these gifts, when it's all said and done, there are going to be holes that one person alone, trying to do all of these things at the same time, will miss.

No one can do it all.

As I look at my own gifts I'm thankful. I am a musician and an artist, and I can connect, to some degree, with teens. But I am unorganized, I can't find my way out of a parking lot, I whine when I don't get my way, and sometimes I ignore people when I'm stressed out—and that's just the tip of the Procopio iceberg.

That's why God has surrounded me with people— volunteer staff. As I peruse my list of volunteers, I see that each one of them has a gift I don't have. It may be organization, incredible phone skills, the ability to listen for a long time, a sense of direction, a love for the most irritating people, one especially who knows how to tell me (in love) to knock off the whining and focus in on the problem, and on and on. I'm gratefully overwhelmed by the different people that God is using to shape me. Some of their giftedness is rubbing off on me, and some of me is rubbing off on them. With each relationship the circular will of God is again cycled, resulting in saints who are a bit more like him and a team that is more deeply committed to the task at hand.

Although our gifts are different, our passion is the same—to see teens become disciples, to watch the love of God grow in young hearts, to witness a rescue from eternal death to eternal life, to behold a metamorphosis from struggling saint to mighty warrior. It doesn't happen with a one-youth-minister show. It happens as we trust God to use the others that he placed in our lives. It happens as we run the race together.

As the three Special Olympic runners pulled ahead, one went down. And although ahead by a comfortable margin, the lead runner stopped in his tracks and turned around to help his comrade. Then the third place runner joined him. They picked up their friend and continued the race, the one in the center being held up by the other two. The three athletes crossed the finish line together, shoulder to shoulder, to the music of a thunderous ovation. In their minds, there was nothing special about their conduct. It was just a race, and their actions on the track simply reflected their passion for the sport, their love and respect for each other. But everyone else present went home with a new appreciation for athletic competition and a deeper sense of what togetherness is all about.

You and your volunteers are racing together. The prize? Young souls. It's good to know that when you stumble, God will be there clothed in the faces of friends, volunteers who believe in you and are willing to help pick you up. You can refuse their help and crawl by them or you can reach out to them and allow them the privilege of holding you up by the arms.

Your call is to help kids carry out the plan of God in their lives.

Your volunteers' call is to carry you. ♡

Great Grace

Sometimes we make grasping the hand of God seem so unattainable. I was observing a prayer time with our kids the other night and I noticed something that caught my attention. One of our eighth graders was praying to beat the band. This kid had had a rough go of it, especially when it came to family matters. As she was praying, I realized that what she was doing was not really praying at all, but striving, wrestling with herself, pleading with God for acceptance. I could almost hear her thoughts as she strained within herself to arrive at a certain place in the spiritual road. "I've got to get this! I've got to get this!"

She exuded a certain hardness, a heaviness, an overwhelming sense that the boat was cruising by and she had to hurry if she wanted to catch it. As I listened I reflected back on my own particular course through which I arrived at my "boat." It was evident that this young girl needed to experience the same miracle of grace.

I had some pretty heavy emotional baggage from all the early orphanage years and the subsequent reuniting with my dad. My entire life as a young boy was consumed with trying to become acceptable enough to a man whose old-world Italian ways didn't allow for affection with his kids. (You should see him now though—he's a pussycat.) I was performing, doing what I had to do, trying to get the love and attention I wanted. And if I didn't get it from dad, I'd get it from others. Hence, my need led me from one situation to another, performing, doing whatever was necessary so I might be accepted and perceived as belonging somewhere.

When I found Christ, I realized love and acceptance like nothing else available in this world. In an instant I went from pauper to prince and none of it was based upon my ability to perform. Nor was I required to jump through religious hoops. All I needed to do was accept the gift of God. The meaning of the cross became clear, and I could finally rest, be myself, and let God do the changing. In short, I'd discovered grace— God's love and acceptance even when we don't deserve it. It was his grace that motivated me to allow him to change me. Discovering God's grace was the single most important event in my life.

I enjoyed this newfound freedom—until I started going to church regularly. I was so much in love with Jesus, I could have been told to stand on my head in church and I would have given it a shot because Jesus had so radically changed my life. What I discovered after attending for a bit was that I had begun performing again—but this time for a different audience. One of the "good brothers" told me that holy people cut their hair, so I did. Another told me that I should stop wearing jeans to church, so I did. Yet another told me that if I really want to be a man of God in the '70s that I needed to wear a leisure suit and, yes, I'm ashamed to say I did. (Shudder.)

The more I got into this church thing, though, the less acceptable I felt to Christ, and one by one I began mounting up a list of self-imposed standards that I felt would make me more acceptable to God. *I have to pray an hour every day. I have to read five chapters of the Bible every day. I have to do this. I can't do that. I must have this look, I must have that thing, etc., etc., etc.* I began adding these things to what Christ did for me on the cross. It was grace plus my prayer time that made me acceptable, the cross plus my outward appearance, grace plus my time studying the Bible, the cross plus this, grace plus that. You could hardly see the cross in my life because of the mountain of religion I had shoveled on top of it.

After several years of *loving* Jesus, I came to the point that I didn't *like* him very much because he was making my life miserable. And I wondered, How did this thing get so muddy?

God must have sensed my misdirection because amid all the confusion, God sent two great people—my wife Rhonda's brother and his wife—to talk some sense into me.

What did they tell me? Their counsel was couched in a question: "Well, Glenn, why are you doing all that stuff?" I was a little offended and probably more than a bit condescending. After all, what would these people know of *my* spiritual walk? They weren't ministers. (Yes, I was an idiot.) "Because I want to be a man of God," I said. "I want his approval on my life. I want to know that my relationship with him is okay."

As bright as the Oklahoma sun that day, their response was a light that pierced the darkness of my good intentions. "Glenn," they said, "that stuff's not going to make you more acceptable to God. You're okay now! You just don't know it. It's Jesus alone that makes us acceptable to God, not all that other stuff."

Talk about feeling stupid. The truth was hidden under six years of religious trappings and yet I finally recognized it once more. I took the plunge into his grace again, remembering how good it was to be forgiven, that I *was* okay and none of it was because of me. All these other things were good, wonderful, marvelous things but, done for the wrong reason, they became chains hobbling my walk with God.

Some ten years later, I heard a hero of mine at a conference workshop. Dave Busby was a youth pastor's youth pastor. His humor, his ability to communicate, and his wonderful transparency endeared him to the hearts of thousands like me. When I sat in on his workshop on "Keys to Long Term Survival," I was expecting practical stuff regarding staff relationships or something like that, but what I received that day was an intimation of grace. Once again, the Holy Spirit did surgery on my soul.

Dave stepped us through his grace journey and, at the end, he gave us words regarding the proper motivation for why we do what we do. I share them with you because they echoed my heart that day. They still do even now.

"I have my quiet times now," he said, "but I don't have them to impress God or get points with him. I don't do it to receive his approval and I don't do it to impress you. I have quiet times with him because I miss Jesus and I want to be with Jesus. He has captured my heart."

We are so concerned with the gospel changing the behavior of our kids that, sometimes, we unwittingly impose a set of standards that can do more harm than good if done for the wrong reasons. Some of our kids are striving with God to be "okay" because they don't know they already *are* okay—and that's a tragedy. They are busy riding a performance treadmill because we've given them the impression that they need to in order to be acceptable to God.

As a youth pastor, I desire the teens in my care to know that *serving* Jesus comes out of *loving* Jesus, not out of trying to make ourselves more likable to him.

David Busby knew of grace. Born with polio, he also fought a daily battle with cystic fibrosis, a lung condition that sapped his stamina and made every day a special gift from his Heavenly Father. In this same session, as he candidly spoke of his condition and related it to walking in grace, he made a statement that will forever be a reminder of why I serve Jesus:

"I think of my condition and after contemplating the way that this thing may play out, I have to tell you, I'm not afraid to die. But one thing terrifies me. And that's *dying before I die*—waking up and realizing that my walk in Christ is lifeless and empty."

Dave went home in December of 1997. But his legacy and ministry live on.

The Christian life is found not in striving but in resting. And that's the good news of the gospel. For your sanity, for your love of God, for the sake of a kid who might be on a performance treadmill, discover grace again. ♡

On Arms

The Civil War diary of Bingham Findlay Junkin reveals the insight of a man of faith and honor and hope. But burrow into its pages and you will find another pearl of counsel that would bear hearing today.

B.F. Junkin was a member of the 100th Pennsylvania Volunteer Infantry. The "Roundheads," as they were called, were heroic men, loyal to their ideals. Bravery was the norm. Reading through the diary of this young husband, you'll find a depth of spiritual wisdom that came from countless hours spent alone with Christ, allowing the truth of God's word and the power of the Holy Spirit to crystallize the image of God within him.

Friday, March 25, 1864

Marched out about three miles to camp which gave us a good appetite for our hard tack. After supper, some of the boys got to dancing and seemed to enjoy themselves right well. I stepped into a cookhouse, sat down by the stove, and endeavored to cast my thoughts on God, ask him to take care of my dear ones at home, keep me and preserve me from evil. Oh, how much grace the Christian soldier needs and how comforting the thought that God reigns everywhere.

The pages are consistently filled with reflections upon his chaplain's Sunday sermons and their prayer meetings on Sunday evening. Even when marching, at every opportunity, a group of men in the 100th company met to worship God and to draw strength from him during this horrendous period in American history.

The soldier recounts various battles and various miracles. How God had spared his life from bullets that flew by near enough for him to feel the wind from them, and cannonballs that landed close enough to almost bury him with dirt yet did not burst. He describes his own conviction with orders to drill on Sundays when they were not engaged in battle:

Sunday, April 10

Sabbath—it rained about daylight, cleared, warm and pleasant. Had a good sermon by Mr. Dickson from Isaiah 55:7. Had prayer meeting in the evening. We had dress parade at five o'clock, 30 minutes, something I think is entirely out of place to thus desecrate the Sabbath. It is a practice which is entirely unnecessary and should be discountenanced by all good men. I have and will continue to speak against, for I think it is very wrong. To ask God's blessing on our army and then willfully disobey him is a mockery. Can we expect a blessing?

From late April 1864 through June, the battles became more frequent, the action more frenzied. Yet even in times of combat, Junkin's faith remained intact. But it's not just his uncommon faith that bears our attention. The next entries listed below contain a common thread that trumpet out a warning to you and me a century later. Although we are in a different conflagration and the enemy we battle is not flesh and blood, the warning is no less important.

Monday, May 9

Started about three in the morning. Marched several different directions, I suppose 10 miles in all. Formed line of battle about 2 o'clock. Again slept on our arms but were not disturbed. Had a good sleep which we needed very much.

Wednesday, May 11

Lay in our ditches til about three o'clock. Then retreated across the Ny branch of the Mattaponi River. Returned to our pits a little after dark and was on guard a part of the night. It rained and we had to sleep on our arms again.

Thursday, May 12

Had coffee and started off for the line of battle. Kept a skirmished fight through the woods during which Joseph [B.F.'s brother] was wounded and Paree was killed. About 2 o'clock we were ordered to make a charge through the woods, but we were soon on a rifle pit and were forced to fall back with heavy loss to our regiment. Company E lost 22 in wounded and killed during the day... We fell back a short distance and lay on our arms all night. Had our skirmishes and ordered not to sleep for fear of a surprise. Rained on us all day and night.

"On arms."

The phrase means that even while the men were resting in their rifle pits or the ditches their hands were not to leave their weapons. When they slept, their rifles were under them. As they watched the blackness of the night creep over them, they were never more than a breath away from drawing fire. Commanders knew that when the battles had subsided and men were at their ease, that's when they were most vulnerable to surprise attack.

Years ago, after surviving the hectic schedule of a Christmas season while doing youth and music ministry in a small church, I thought I could again breathe. It had been a difficult season. Between the holiday music program and the youth ministry, it had been a maddening month. I was tired, burned out, and looking forward to a few weeks to take it easy. My guard was down, so needless to say, I was totally blindsided when the pastor told me the next day after the Christmas program, "They're nipping at your heels, Glenn." He was referring to a small group of malcontents who didn't care much for me.

I'm not so naive as to think that everyone would always think I was doing a perfect job. But up to that point, I had always found a way to coexist with others even when we disagreed. This would not be such a situation, however. The pastor was behind me, I had his support, but he let me know that I'd probably never be able to win these people over. Although I should have chalked up the situation to experience, this thing really bothered me, in fact, consumed me. For weeks I was unable to sleep, tempted to just throw in the towel.

After a tough schedule when I expected to rest, when fatigue had set in and emotional burnout was around the corner, I should have been "on arms." I've learned long ago that the enemy doesn't fight fair. I also know that some of his most devious plans are those in which he uses good people whom he manipulates. I tell my kids this all the time, and yet there I was, in the throes of one of the most difficult trials of my life. I was being attacked by a maneuver of spiritual forces and didn't realize it. Had I been spiritually prepared, the situation could have been easily understood and resisted; but I wasn't, and the depression I experienced was severe.

Had I been "on arms," it would have strengthened my resolve in prayer rather than weakening it. Had I been "on arms," I would have leaned more heavily on the Lord rather than blaming him for my problem. Had I been "on arms," I would have sensed his hand holding me up and undergirding me rather than feeling a spiritual weight choking the life out of me.

"On arms." I know I'm sharing no new revelation. I realize that we all know the dangers of unpreparedness. But in retrospect I wonder if we can understand the depth of its blessing when we *are* "on arms."

B.F. Junkin learned that his brother was shot during the battle of Spotsyvania. During the days that followed he was unable to learn any details about his brother. The agony of not knowing would have been enough to consume a normal person. But "on arms" in the middle of battle, the urgency of the fight at hand keeps our mind and heart focused on the enemy, forging ahead. His entries reflect the power of preparedness. We see a man not destroyed by the events but strengthened in his faith.

Sunday, May 15

Sabbath generally quiet along the line except for some picket firing. We have been in here five days, raining most of the time, more or less, but notwithstanding the exposure and danger to which we are exposed, "The Lord has been very gracious to me in preserving my health and sparing my life."

Monday, May 16

Nothing of note occurred. We still hold our pits and keep out our skirmishers. I did hear that Joseph had died of his wound, but am not certain of the truth of it yet.

Tuesday, May 17

Lay on the watch as usual. Nothing occurred on the line worthy of note. Met with Hugh Means in the evening who informed me that a Mr. Dickson told him that Joseph died. How true, "that in the midst of Life we are in death."

One week later as the battle rages on, his entry reads one more exhortation.

Wednesday, May 25

Were sent on out from the skirmish line. Shot at and was shot at by the Rebs but by the infinite mercy of God, my life was spared, although the bullets came frequently near me, but in God alone is our help to be found.

Bingham Junkin suffered a gunshot in the right thigh on June 17 which shattered his hip bone, and still his life was spared. After struggling with recovery, he was given an honorable discharge on July 8, 1865, and lived to be 78 years old. He died on May 11, 1911.

We, too, are on the front lines. We can't afford the luxury of not being "on arms" even for a bit. But the blessing of preparedness is that, even during the most pressing of circumstances, *in God alone is our help to be found.*

It was true for B.F Junkin. It's true for us, too. ♡

The Diary of B.F. Junkin *is archival material under the curatorship of Eric and Elizabeth Davis in Columbus, Ohio. The full archive may be viewed online at* http://www.iwaynet.net/~lsci/junkin/index.htm

The Price of Pride

2 Chronicles 26

Azariah and his 80 other priests had no idea what would happen when they confronted the king. It was a risky move. Most of them had read of the power of God but had probably never seen the hand of God come against the monarchy in an instant of divine wrath. What, if anything, would God do?

Uzziah had started so well, going farther in his reforms than his father Amaziah. Uzziah was determined not to have any other gods in Israel. This nation was as unfaithful as it was moody, one moment lifting up praises, the next bowing before idols. Uzziah had seen it all. At age 16, he took the throne with steel-jawed determination, vowing that this time things would be different.

And that doesn't surprise me. Have you ever see a teen get fired up about something then turned loose? You'd sooner stop the tide than deter them. Give up? Ain't gonna happen. Uzziah was sick to death of all the unfaithfulness. He remembered the image of his own father bowing to strange gods. That image kindled a fire for doing right that pushed Uzziah until a radical wave of God-consciousness swept Israel.

Then God granted him favor in his military. Army after army was defeated by this kid who had enough wisdom to consult God and enough backbone to depend upon him. His armies were soon feared in all the land and a renewed respect for Israel began to grow. He released the creative energy of machinists and soon the city was fortified with the latest state-of-the-art catapults and arrow launchers. Like a ground-swell of hope, the people began to believe that a leader from David's mold was on the throne.

Uzziah's style? If something needed to be done, then he'd expect it to be done and done right. I can imagine him in a board meeting. Right was right. It's my way or the highway. Let's compromise—do it my way. And while he was humble before the Lord, he could do it with confidence because as long as he was consulting God, his way *was* the right way.

But somewhere along the line, Uzziah got off track. The scripture is unclear about what made the difference. What it does say is that after Uzziah became powerful, his "pride led to his downfall."

He blew it in a well-intentioned thought—noble in Uzziah's mind. Uzziah tried to place himself in the office of priest and offer incense to the Lord, something that only a descendant of Aaron could do. The "take the bull by the horns" mentality had finally taken him across the line. Notice Uzziah's response and you'll see what separated him from David. Unlike David, who was broken and repentant when confronted by his failure, Uzziah got angry at the priests for interfering. "Who are you to tell me what to do?" he yelled.

Funny thing about pride. It's slippery when you try to nail down the problem with it. The problem is not this act or that act. It's that pride takes first place in the heart. No one gets prideful who hasn't enjoyed at least some measure of success, even in a limited capacity. The Bible is full of examples—Saul, Uzziah's father Amaziah, Hezekiah, and more. All these men started out by trusting, but soon they were haunted by the consequences of a prideful heart. Their trust and dependence *on* him led to a presumption *of* him. Kind of a dangerous thing to do.

Before we go righteously clucking too loud, we probably ought to examine our own hearts. Pride is the one thing that will destroy our ministry without our knowledge. There are no clear dividing lines when it comes to pride, the boundaries become increasingly gray. When pride sneaks in, we become good at manipulating our own motives, stubbornly believing that we are still on track spiritually when inside we're dying. It's a dangerous fog to be in, this fog of pride.

And it was a high price to pay for Uzziah.

As he was ranting and raving at the priests, a white spot appeared on his forehead. Azariah knew what it was immediately. Leprosy. What a perfect parallel. For as leprosy eats away the skin, leaving stench and decay, so pride ruins any godly influence that we may have, giving others a foul impression of what's on the inside of our hearts.

Ask a kid who's been raked over the coals by an overzealous youth leader who can never say, "Hey, I was wrong." Ask a kid who's been hurt by a leader who is good at condemning and bad at grace. Ask a kid who is afraid to ask his or her youth leader for help for fear of the reaction—a condescending roll of the eyes and a patronizing voice with a silent "I told you so" attached to every word.

When pride is present in a leader, the message dies.

One moment Uzziah was a self-starter king who wasn't going to be told what to do by a bunch of high-minded priests. The next he was being escorted out of the temple and into self-imposed banishment, filled with a painful reminder of just how destructive pride can be. He spent his last days alone, separated from the people he loved and robbed of the influence that made him truly distinct. Leprosy was the price for a prideful spirit.

One cannot be sure of how his pride influenced God's hand upon Israel, but it is interesting to note Isaiah's words, how the Lord revealed himself *after* Uzziah had left the scene.

"In the year that King Uzziah died, I saw also the Lord, high and lifted up..." Isaiah 6:1

When pride died, the people saw God again. ♡

Nursing Your Wounds

I've never considered myself much of a fighter. In the fights that I had as a kid, I never fared too well. As a 14-year-old, I wasn't much to look at—literally. I was five foot nine and weighed something less than 90 pounds. A bag of bones with a mouth. My younger brother Bobby, on the other hand, was my size, had 30 pounds on me, and could beat a grizzly one-handed on a bad night. So I skirted trouble with him by talking my way out of it, most of the time.

This incident is not one of those times. My brother's mission in life was to make me miserable and he went after it with abandon. Most of the time I could ignore him or make him feel ridiculous when he got on my nerves, but this day was different. As I was looking in my dresser for something, he came up behind me and, three inches from my ear, began to say "You're stupid, Glenn. You're stupid, Glenn. You're stupid, Glenn," over and over again. I kept my composure through the first 60 stanzas, but after he took another breath and began again, something snapped. Now I've never been a particularly courageous individual, so I attribute my actions that day to a momentary lapse of common sense.

In a move that I remember happening in slow motion, my right hand balled into a fist, and with all the inertia that my slender build could muster, I spun as fast as I could and brought my fist up squarely under his jaw. As uppercuts go, it was a thing of beauty, lifting him ever so briefly off his feet and onto the bed. For a millisecond that seemed to last hours, he was out.

I threw my fists into the air in a dance that would have made Sylvester Stallone proud. I began revelling in the newfound respect that my brother was sure to have for me now. Boy, I was dreaming.

In retrospect I did two things wrong that day. First, I should never have hit him in the first place. Second, I didn't run when I had the chance. When he woke a second later, he looked like something out of the Tasmanian Devil cartoon—his fists and feet were everywhere and they were all over me. I was no Einstein back then, but when I began seeing little white spots in my eyes, I knew that I wasn't winning this one. I collapsed in a heap. My nose was evenly dispersed over my face, my right eye was bloody, and my lips were swollen shut. It wasn't a red-letter day for my fighting career, that's for sure.

I found my bearings a few minutes later. I was downstairs, holding an ice pack on my nose and lips, and I was crying. This wasn't a tantrum cry, this was a cry when you were hurting, the kind that sounds like stifled sneezes. Every inhalation of breath was another convulsion for my chin and swollen lips. Blubbering, I was humiliated and embarrassed.

Try as hard as I could, I just couldn't stop. The harder I tried, the more difficult it became to get my composure. My dad, in his deeply understanding Italian way, comforted me: "STOP THE CRYING. NOW!" I guess he figured that the shock value thing would work in this case. It didn't; I blubbered worse.

At that point, my stepmother stepped in. ("Stepmother" is a bad title for her. She was the only real mom I ever knew, and if sainthood was awarded for loving someone else's kid, she'd be next in line.) "He doesn't need to be yelled at!" she said, and reached her arms around me and hugged me tightly. She had hugged me before, but none have stayed in my memory like that one. In that embrace was comfort, love, and a sense of security that calmed me instantly. The sobs grew quiet, the tears stopped, and for twenty minutes or so she cleared the kitchen and she just held me. I don't ever remember that happening before, and a doctor's prescription could not have been more powerfully effective.

I wasn't her biological child. But at that moment, no maternal instinct was ever stronger. This was her son, and she was taking care of me, comforting, nursing my wounds, and calming me down.

I remember that incident a lot. Mostly because it's such a great memory, but also because in ministry you get beat up a lot from various directions. There will always be those who want you to be in a different mold or have a different approach to ministry, to be more conventional, to not play such loud music on youth group nights—whatever. Sometimes they are minor skirmishes, other times they're bloody battles.

When I was teaching at a church-school in Detroit, I was treated to a verbal beating from a set of parents. Without going into the specifics, I was absolutely right in my position but was also trying to be sensitive to them. So I kept silent, not defending myself, just letting them vent. I should have felt okay about it when they left, but I didn't. I was hurt, deeply wounded. Even knowing I was right did nothing to soothe the war that was going on inside me. I wasn't thinking of giving up or quitting, but these people had opened a hole in my gut.

I wish I could say that there was a verse or a sermon or a friend who came on the scene and made the situation better. It didn't happen. Truth was, the wounds were deep and I realized that I'd probably hurt for some time. However, I could sense God comforting me, and the mental image that appeared in my mind was that of my stepmom—my mom— years earlier.

Like my mom, his arms around my soul didn't make the swelling go down or lessen the pain, but he did help my soul to stop sobbing. Although hurting, my soul was at peace. Although wounded, my heart was not in panic.

Read these words and let the reality of God's presence soothe you if you are hurting. If you aren't, put these words in the bank for a later time, for sooner than you may realize you'll need to hear them again. Let the words be a balm to your wounds and let his presence help the sobbing in your soul to subside. You may have to deal with the effects of whatever your particular hurt is for some time, but as you nurse your wounds, there God is, allowing you the privilege to rest in his care until the wounds are healed and you can again face the battle.

And when you are ready to fight the fight of faith once more, he'll stand with you.

After my fighting incident was over, I never quite saw Mom the same way. She always stood taller, always seemed to beam brighter. The same is true with our God. When you've tasted the soothing of his presence in your trouble, when he has comforted you through a dark night in your soul, your walk will be sweeter, more intimate. For he has seen you at your most vulnerable and you have allowed him access to your hurt.

The fights we have we may not always win, but if we allow his arms to soothe us, every fight we survive will make us stronger. ♡

Storm Survivors

Never had a bride looked more lovely. Mandie came down the aisle that day beaming so beautifully even her wedding dress seemed to glow. As her husband-to-be escorted her onto the platform and they said their vows together, I began to realize that this kid was a storm survivor. She was beginning her life as a beautiful bride, her radiance burning through the storms she had weathered as a teen.

I first met Mandie when I came to Yakima, Washington as a new youth pastor. She was a cute 13-year-old who was all smiles, bubbles, and witty remarks. She was also a gymnast and she was good—world-class good. Shortly after I arrived, she'd had an accident at one of her gymnastic camps. A crushed vertebrae. She had been rushed to a specialist in Seattle. This was not good. Thus began a harrowing ordeal in and out of hospitals, through recovery, reinjury, and recovery again. For all but one surgery, I was there in the waiting room with her mom. Procedure after procedure over a period of years finally resulted in a metal rod inserted in her back.

Mandie's faith was a study in contrasts, one moment strong as the Rock of Gibraltar, and the next, flimsy and eggshell thin. I seriously had my doubts about whether Mandie's faith would survive. I'd seen kids more solid than she falter at far less. But she hung in there.

The day finally came during her last surgery when she was told by the doctor that she would never compete again. It was a tough conversation. If anything was gonna push her over the edge, this would do it. When the doctor left, she cried quietly, silently resigning herself to the fact that Olympic dreams would remain just that—dreams. She also knew that any career in the sport would be relegated to the sidelines.

As she cried, the storm raged. She asked why and we tried to make sense of it, but during the storm you don't make sense of it—you comfort and try to help the friend through. You help them see that the storms are a part of life. You try to point them to the one who knows the storm's intensity far better than anyone else.

In the early maritime days of sailing vessels, storms at sea were challenges that a ship's captain had to face regularly. Though most storms were manageable, a wise captain also knew when it was time to set the sails into the wind and let the direction of the storm determine the course—hence the term *riding out the storm*. Riding out the storm often meant a new course bearing and a new destination when the storm was over, but knowing when to ride out the storm was the difference between a wise captain and a foolish one. It also meant the difference between storm casualties and storm survivors.

Spiritual storm survivors are wise captains. Because of the many storms, they come to know when to fight the storm and when to ride it out. Having life shaped by the storms is what makes them what they are—ready to resist yet knowing when to go with the storm, letting the pain of it determine direction for the future.

Jesus was a storm survivor, too. You can hear the words of a wise captain in his words at the garden of Gethsemane: *"Peter, put away your sword. Shall I not drink of the cup that the Father has given me to drink?"* After a night in Gethsemane, in the raging storm of facing Calvary, Jesus could ride out his storm because he knew that his father had things in hand. After agonizing over the decision, Jesus finally allowed God to use the storm of the cross to determine the direction of humanity.

Is the storm raging? Have you been fighting the wind for so long that you hardly know how to let go? It may be time for you to "ride out your storm." It may be time to stop fighting it, to humbly place yourself at the mercy of the storm, allowing the Father to use it to produce godliness in you. Rather than firing off a letter of rebuke, season your words with love. Rather than stiffening your neck and setting your jaw as you enter the meeting, ask God to simply produce the peaceable fruit of righteousness in you. Instead of raking your kids over the coals for not being the kind of group that makes you proud, lead them in repentence, beginning the process yourself.

Storm survivors are those whose faith is shaped not during times of calm, but in hard times, when things are at their worst. For so many in ministry, storms come as total surprises. With the wind and the rain comes our cry to the Lord to take the storm away, blind to the fact that with each storm comes a new possibility of learning mastery over it—but also learning, when necessary, to let the storm do its work, even if painful.

My message at Mandie's wedding to her and her husband was actually a card, a 25th wedding anniversary card. I read it to them and instructed them to read it again when the big day rolled around in 25 years. As I looked into Mandie's eyes that day, I silently relived every storm this kid and I shared. I remembered and, of course, cried. With all that she faced, she survived, and God's righteousness was produced in her.

The very power of the storm that makes it so frightening may enable you to lean on the power of the Lord, making you, too, a storm survivor. ♡

The Power of Fun

Manly specimens of humanity took their places on the field of battle—faces stern with determination, minds focused on the game ahead. The gridiron was thick with the heavy emotion of the moment. Two teams faced each other, ready to do competitive battle. Jaws were set, eyes narrowed as they readied themselves for the kickoff. The crowd was still. Not a sound was in the air as the two armies awaited the beginning of the game. Suddenly the silence was broken by a lone cry: "Hey! You guys got one more than our team!"

The back-to-school retreat had just begun. As we awaited dinner, a game of football had developed. I was new in the church and at my first big function. I already had pictures of each of the 130 kids in the group and had even memorized every name. I was on top of it. Things were hopping. I had high hopes for this retreat, and I wanted every event to be a winner. As I realized the football dilemma, I sauntered over to Matt. Matt's an intelligent kid, a computer whiz, a sensitive person with a gift for common sense and the ability to articulate himself that is way beyond his 15 years.

But he wasn't a jock and, because of that, he often felt left out of place at things like this. Still, I had a nagging feeling that he could benefit from the experience, so I egged him toward the game and the other guys took him in. It was a game of light tackle with what we call a "five, one thousand" rush. As the game started, Matt did okay. He wasn't after a Heismann, but he held his own and wasn't embarrassed.

Then it was Matt's team's turn to play defense, and they put Matt in to rush. He squatted down in a three-point stance, ready to slow down any defender off the line. As the ball was snapped, I could hear Matt's voice above all others barking the cadence for the impending rush, "one

one thousand, two one thousand, three....five one thousand." I still see it in slow motion. Never was effort more profoundly rewarded. With a swipe of his arms, Matt threw the defender out of the way and in five quick steps had the quarterback sacked. It was a thing of beauty and Matt arose a hero. He heard the cheers of his peers, and from the look on his face, I knew it was the first time he'd ever had them.

As I share these words, I realize that things don't always end up that way. I know that sometimes when you encourage a kid to hop into something new, it backfires. I know that we have to be careful when we encourage kids to step too far out of their comfort zones. But this time, for Matt, it was right on the mark, and that incident immediately set the tone for our relationship.

Fun is an important element in connecting with kids—not the only one certainly, but an important one nonetheless. I see new guys entering the youth ministry field and, as I look into their eyes, I can categorize them in a heartbeat. There are those who enter youth ministry because they consider it a cool job. There are those who are entering youth ministry on their way to something else. And there are those who want the job because they love the thought of God actually using them to touch kids.

All three of these groups have a different idea of what youth ministry is, but one thing they have in common is that they believe it's going to be fun—and it is. But it's a dangerous assumption to think that the majority of what a youth worker does is fun-filled.

Bus trips are aggravating. Details matter. Paperwork is boring. Meetings are necessary. And believe it or not, the kids sometimes can be a pain. It's not all fun, yet the fun is a tool that God uses to chip away at each soul.

Wise youth ministry is that which uses fun to open the heart up to relationship but uses love to share the good news of the gospel. I've seen the power of fun work many times in a wonderful domino effect: The fun of a game or an activity. Smiles and laughter. A newfound friendship. An open heart. An obedient servant. A message shared. A willing soul. A decision. A new soul enters the kingdom.

There are those who sneer at fun. I can respect that. I will be the first to show my respect for a brother who has no sense of spiritual humor. I'll even put my arm around his shoulder. (Of course, I'm normally taping a "kick me" sign to them at the same time.) These people think that God has no sense of humor. C'mon, I want to say—

Do you honestly think that Balaam didn't laugh himself out of his saddle after his donkey spoke to him?

Can you tell me that Peter didn't bust a gut when, after an angel released him from prison, the maid slammed the door in his face thinking he was a ghost?

Don't you think that Jesus enjoyed watching the disciples squirm whenever he asked them a tough spiritual question?

God loves fun. He wants us to use it as we minister to teens. The power of fun is that it disarms people of their verbal weapons and their destructive attitudes. Words can't do in a year what laughter can do in a few minutes.

A word of advice to you. Lighten up. Laugh.

Some kid is waiting to open up to you if only they can see you laugh. And more importantly, there are kids in your group who haven't laughed in quite some time. It's through tickling their funny bones that you may very well touch their hearts.

How powerful is fun, anyway? Ask a kid named Matt who decided to let his guard down, have some fun, and walked away a hero. Ask the youth pastor who's seen him grow. And ask God who smiles and laughs with glee when he sees it happen in you. ♡

"I Wanna Go Wif You"— A Longing for Connection

Although over three decades have passed, the words still echo in my mind as if the moment had just happened.

"I wanna go wif you..."

Because of a split-up of our home four years earlier, my brothers, my sister, and I were sent to two different orphanages—the older kids going to St. Mary's in Nashville, and my younger brothers (Bobby and Tony) and I were placed in St. Peters in Memphis.

Tony was just a baby when we arrived, I was three, and Bobby was two.

When we started school, we were sent to a different section of the compound and, although separated, we still saw a lot of each other. We grew up together, managed to stay close, and although my memories are clouded, I can still see Tony as I did the last day we saw each other.

Bobby and I were to be sent to St. Marys to join our other siblings, and I had to tell Tony that we would be leaving. He sat on the steps by the pool, feet dangling in the water, the sun glistening off the perspiration peeking through his blond brush-cut hair. Though a lump was in my throat, I told him that he would be joining us later (I was assuming). "But I wanna go wif you." It wouldn't be long, I said. "But I wanna go wif you." I would write letters and send pictures, I said. I hugged him, sloppily tried to wipe a tear from his eye, and smiled. I didn't know what else to do.

The wrought-iron fence around the pool gave an unusual coldness to the hot summer day. As I looked back, I saw him through the black bars, still sitting on the steps, face in hands. That is my last memory of him. A five-year-old boy trying to cope with emotions too complex for most adults to imagine.

We learned later that Tony had been adopted out to a military family, probably a pretty good home, a great opportunity. But in a secret corner of my heart there is always this dull ache, a longing to know how he's doing or what he grew up to be. I never did find out. I just know that seldom a week goes by without my mind wandering into the world of "what if" or "might have been." There's a longing for a missing connection that I can't explain.

It's an awful lot like my relationship with God.

I long for connection. A far-off ache within my soul cries out for relationship—a relationship that is deeper than what I am experiencing now. I could go for days and weeks feeling that God could never be closer, but I always find myself longing, aching for a deeper walk, a more substantial connection to the one who makes my life make sense.

At times, I am amazed at my shallowness.

I'm amazed that I can be so authoritative and confident and sure of myself only to turn around and act petty and selfish and insecure. It's during those periods that I am acutely aware that I am a very needy person.

And I feel that dull ache again. I want to throw myself at his feet, telling him "Not my way, God—I wanna go with you."

Each of us brings our own brand of idiosyncrasies and neuroses into the ministry with us. It's precisely these things that have made us the type of caregivers we are. But the singular reason that we have been given this extraordinary calling is because there is that longing, that dull ache within us, the one that drives us to our knees proclaiming our desire to know him more deeply and that we are desperately inadequate without him.

This past year my family and I were driving through Memphis on our way back home from vacation. On a whim I looked up St. Peters. It's still there. St. Judes bought the property and was readying it for renovation, so we drove over. I was amazed by its smallness. I found the rooms that I had described to my wife in detail, the gray-green wall tiles launching me into the memory world of distant time.

And I saw the pool. Although surrounded by a tall wooden fence with a locked gate, I peered through the slats. The iron fence is gone, but the steps are still there. And through the half-inch crack I saw a little kid with a brush cut staring back at me, wanting to go with me.

Tony is a man now, probably with a family of his own. Although my memories of him are few, his last words to me became a prayer, for these are the words I say to God when I feel the longing for connection to the one whose death made my life possible:

"Not my way, God—I wanna go with you."

"That I might know him, and the power of his resurrection, and the fellowship of his sufferings..." Philippians 3:10 KJV ♡

Seeds of Change

Outside the Detroit Rescue Mission, a man was slapping his wife. An argument resulted in an act of violence that was one-sided and over with before anyone could do anything about it.

I had taken a group of forty or so kids to Detroit on a ministry trip. At the mission, the group was busy doing various duties, and through the experience they were stretched beyond their middle-class world. To this day, when reflecting back on the trip, the day at the mission was where their most vivid memories were made.

During a break between jobs, Melanie was headed to our bus when she saw the couple outside the fence of the mission. It was there that she received her first taste of the raw brutality of domestic violence. I was in the back of the mission scrubbing some cans, when I caught her out of the corner of my eye, standing at the fence, crying.

At this time in her life, Melanie had yet to indicate a real serious desire in her faith. She had experienced God on a basic level, but there was an aloofness to her relationship with Christ and, at times, a defiance. That quality would either separate her as a woman of God or ultimately lead to her rebellion. I had always worried about Mel just a little.

When I saw her crying, I went out and asked what was wrong. She couldn't talk at first. When she did, her description of the incident she'd witnessed was accented by her sniffles. And through her sobs of hurt and anger and frustration, I realized what had really happened:

A seed of change had been planted.

While watching the violent reality before her, Mel was also playing her own life before her eyes. She realized how fortunate she was, and a silent—maybe even subconscious—self-evaluation was taking place.

While trying to understand the *whys* of the situation, the Holy Spirit was breaking up the fallow ground in her soul. God had decided to make her heart ripe for the seed of change. Her deep sobs reflected the depth of the furrow that God was preparing. For Mel, things would have to be different. For her heart, there was no choice.

As we discussed it, I was deeply moved and another sublime memory was added to the treasure chest of my heart.

Although it is difficult to understand the detail which God puts into it, his spirit is ever seeking those opportunities, through people met or situations faced, to change his people. There is not one person a kid meets, not one situation a teen experiences, however minute, that God is not intricately concerned with. Even through wrong choices, God is there, looking for opportunities to drop seeds of truth that might ultimately harvest his will in their lives.

Much of our time in youth ministry is spent planting seeds.

That's why those bus trips are important, because as you are goofing off with them, you are planting the seeds of relationship that will eventually allow you deeper access to their lives.

That's why the calls in the middle of the night aren't a bother, because the care we give during times of confusion are seeds of dependability that will blossom into the flowers of maturity.

That's why even if the kid doesn't know Christ in a personal way, I can plant seeds of love at their school, so that when the time is right and the ground is fertile, I can see it happen. I will have a chance to see the seed bud into faith.

The seeds of faith come in a thousand varieties. Each one produces a different fruit but all effect change. While most of our efforts will be rewarded by seeing growth, there are times that we don't get to see the harvest. Many times kids are grown up and married before we realize that the seeds we planted have bloomed. But that's okay. God hasn't called you to effect the change but to plant the seed.

Two years after our trip to the mission, our group is in the middle of a major move of God. You know where Mel is? Right in the middle of it. The seed of change planted in Detroit has been watered by the Holy Spirit and it is growing.

By the way, look around you. As you drop seeds into their lives, others are dropping them in yours as well. The Lord is breaking up the fallow ground of your heart. Watch those seeds grow. ♡

Dark Clouds, Bright Hopes

I was busy getting stuff together for our weekly youth church when I received Gloria's call. Her brother-in-law had died. It'd be easy for someone who didn't know the story to say, "Sorry about that," and not think a whole lot about it.

So let me tell you the story:

Gloria Rodriguez is a beautiful kid. She came to our group from California about a year and a half ago. The home she left was difficult and abusive, and coming to live with her sister was her last-ditch attempt to find sanity in her mind and peace in her soul. The first Sunday morning she came, her heart melted before the Lord, and during Sunday School she became a Christian.

She fit with this family. They couldn't really afford another mouth to feed. Their finances were stretched tighter than a drum but, through scrimping, they managed somehow to make it. She grew in the Lord and for the first time in her life, she felt like a part of a real family. My own history enabled me to relate, so her joys were my own. That's why the news of her sister's husband having cancer was a shock. In no time he went from bad to worse.

It's now the Saturday of the funeral. In a couple of hours, I will mourn with a family who has lost the glue to their family unit, and I somehow will have to find words to comfort a kid whose heart is breaking.

It's not just that someone close to her has died. It's the baggage that's attached—the fact that this teen has the impression that there is a dark cloud following her. I could hear it in her voice as I talked to her a couple of weeks ago: "What do I have to do to get a break, Glenn? Everything I touch falls apart." How do you find words to comfort a kid who thinks that wherever she goes, disaster is going to follow? How do you look into the woeful eyes of one of God's own and tell her that there's a silver lining behind *this* cloud, and *this* one, and even the next one, too?

Paul had his share of dark days. I'm sure there were mornings when he looked up at the dark cloud and wondered, too. But when encouraging his young protégé, Timothy, he gives us some insight to help those in our care get out from under the dark clouds hanging overhead. As he was speaking of the hardships he endured in his second letter to Timothy, Paul gives him a promise: *"If we suffer, we will also reign with Him."*

The promise is not a bit of pie-in-the-sky-by-and-by word magic. It was a promise intended to motivate a young pastor to keep holding on, to keep being faithful, to endure. Paul's words to Timothy are a rock to stand on, not just when this life is over, but for here and now. It's a cry to all who are called by God's name.

It's in suffering that we learn how to reign.

It's in weeping that we learn how to rejoice.

It's in enduring hardship that we learn to be faithful.

Your kids have heard all the great promises of modern-day Christianity. What they haven't heard is that sometimes it hurts. When bad things happen—what then?

What happens is that God places people in our lives to help us through the valley of the hurt. He uses those people to be umbrellas of protection from the dark clouds above. He uses people to show us that if we suffer in this life, we can still rule over the pain, that it need not consume us.

He uses people to continually point us to Christ and away from the pain. The same cross that provides for our sin is also the cross that endears Christ to us because he suffered so much on it. When he says "I feel your pain," it's not a slogan, it's a fact. And it makes him closer, more intimately involved with our own hurts. When our gaze is fixed steadfastly on what happened to Christ on the cross and why, we quicken our pace toward it in our own growth and, along the way, we pull fellow-sufferers with us.

So right now, my job is to hold a spiritual umbrella over a kid who I know is going to make it—a kid who might be under a dark cloud, but ultimately has a brighter hope, a promise to reign in this life.

My comfort given to her now becomes God's comfort to an unknown someone in the future. For one day Gloria will draw on this experience and she will remember to hold an umbrella for someone else. ♡

God of My Emptiness

Elisha came into the clearing and immediately sensed that something was wrong. The home had always been a haven during his itinerant travels, and over the years he had become very close with the family who lived there. He studied the scene: Shutters tightly closed. No chickens scurrying. The only sign of life was the faint smoke coming from the chimney.

Finally, the woman of the house appeared through the door and cried out to him. Elisha had known her husband and the relationship had been a good one. He had shared meals with this family before and was sad to hear from her about her husband's death. But that was not the reason for her cries. Debt was the reason. The creditors were on their way to get their money or take her son as payment. Wanting desperately to help, Elisha asked "What do you have?" "Not much," she answered, "a little oil is all."

His instructions were strange, to say the least, but the widow had seen God work before through this traveler. So she followed the instructions to the letter.

Isn't it amazing how we react when we're under pressure? My wife tells me that I get this "look" when I'm stressed. The point is that we "spiritual leaders" sometimes become emotional basketcases when we are facing the stresses of ministry. When I'm really stressed, even my prayers reflect it. "Okay, God, here's the deal. You gotta do this thing, because I went out on a line for you, blah, blah, blah—" I sometimes get the feeling that when I am into my problems like that, God would love to pour a bucket of water on me and say, "Chill out!"

It's taken a great bit of hardship and patience for me to realize something very important. When I am stressed out, the best thing I can offer God is *not* my ideas, my help, my services, or even my promise to do better. The *best* thing I can offer God when I'm stressed or anxious is my emptiness.

The widow did as Elisha instructed. She got alone. She gathered as many empty vessels as she could find. And she began to pour. The first few jars were easy because there were places to put them. But after the stacked jars were beginning to fill up, the task became more difficult. You can hear her cries as she told her son, "I need more emptiness, I need more emptiness." As long as there was emptiness available, the oil flowed. Once every vessel was filled, the widow sold the oil. But the lesson she learned about God's faithfulness was worth far more than cash.

The work we do is demanding. Ministry to kids consumes us if we have hearts at all for the work. It's easy to be overwhelmed, easy to be caught simply trying to keep up. It's easy to get frustrated or become demanding. It's easy also to try to barter with God. But he isn't into deals. We have nothing he wants—except our emptiness. What makes us youth leaders is not us, it's him. There are a thousand traps that the enemy sets for youth leaders, and most start and finish with "I." "*I* really should apply for a bigger position. *I* really need a bigger salary. He can't talk to *me* like that. *I* could do better than that, etc., etc., etc." Yet the best any of us can do to find relief is to ask God to crush our will and make it his, to empty ourselves in order to be filled.

About three weeks or so after finding Christ, I experienced the emptying I speak of. At the time I didn't fully understand it, because everything in Christianity was so new to me. During a prayer time in our church I began to cry. I hadn't cried since I was a boy. Even when I became a Christian, I didn't cry—I was extremely happy. I knew it was real but I just didn't cry. The night weeks later, however, was totally different, and my new feelings were linked to the words in a favorite old hymn of mine called "Draw Me Nearer." We don't sing it very much anymore, I've noticed, but privately, I still hear it as a prayer that echoes from the canyons of my heart and from the memory of this night: "*Consecrate me now to thy service Lord by the power of Grace divine. / Let my soul look up with a steadfast hope and my will be lost in thine.*"

No praise chorus could ever sound as good. These words created a knot in my soul that I could not reconcile until I was positive I would walk away empty of self. As I got into my car that evening, I was still crying. I got home and quickly scooted upstairs because I didn't understand why these words could affect me so. Finally, I understood I was empty and I needed to be filled with that power, with that divine will and steadfast hope. And being so became my goal.

Emptiness is a rare commodity today. But I want my kids to see it in me. All that I am, I am because of him, and it just wouldn't seem right for me to lay claim to the work he did. So I visit this widow's house often in the scriptures, asking to become empty, listening to the voice of the spirit speaking quietly to my soul. "I need more emptiness! I need more emptiness!" And when I do, just as the new Christian I was, rare is the time I don't find a lump in my throat. It's a humbling thing to empty yourself out.

But the joy of being filled with the essence of God's heart is worth far more than you will ever be able to pay. ♡

A Word to the Enemy

Satan, I'd like to talk with you. It's time that you, the father of lies, listen for once. I'm putting you on notice:

No longer will you hinder the work of God in my life. No longer will I be a slave to the lies you have whispered in my ears, even the ones from well-meaning people who were just as confused and deceived as I was.

For years I have seen you deceive the young minds of my world. I have seen your handiwork etched in the faces of teens convinced that there is nothing else after this life. I, too, was deceived...but no more.

You tried to ruin me by telling me I was a failure and that I could not change. But I've come to know that my failures are not final. Yes, as a human I have failed before and I am likely to fail again. But hear me, lord of darkness: Even in my failure, the God of heaven that defeated you on the cross will bear me up, offering a way of escape and the opportunity to be changed—to be different—to be more like Christ after the failure than I was before. And I will *never* give up.

You have tried to poison my attitude with thoughts of mistrust and rebellion. You've tried to tell me that my attitude was just a natural by-product of who I am and that changing my attitude was like changing my genetic code. But sell that sales pitch elsewhere. I am wise to you— *my attitude is a choice.* I am aware that even though the world around me falls apart, I can still rejoice, I can still stand and lift up my soul to him who does all things well, knowing that, even in stressful and difficult times, "It is God who works in me, both to will, and to do of his good pleasure."

You have tried to discourage me by overwhelming me through a variety of difficulties. At times I have cried out to God asking where he was. But through every situation I have faced, I have come to learn it's not what happens to me that counts, but what happens *in* me. So give it your best shot, evil one—nothing comes against me that does not pass through Christ's hands first, and he sees my troubles and will deliver me out of them all.

You have tried your best to make me rebel against the limitations placed before me, making me strain at them, and desirous of being free from their confinement. However, through the many turns and twists in my journey, I now know that *limitations are guidelines, not stop signs,* and with each limitation, the hand of the Father has taken me down a new and glorious road.

Your efforts to discourage and distract me, though sometimes compelling, have failed. Problems used to be the source of untold agonies and tears, and during those times I could almost sense your joy in my despair. But as I reflect on my journey, I now realize that *every problem has a hidden possibility* if only I am wise enough to look for it.

Over the years of trying to win young souls, I have witnessed your work, your destruction of teens' minds, your efforts to wipe out a generation and remove their influence from our world.

But look, Satan. Do you see? It is an army of young people taking your kingdom by storm. Who's leading them, you ask? It's me and thousands of others like me, who know that you are defeated and are going to come tumbling down.

Listen, Satan. Do you hear? It's the sound of genuine repentence and truthful worship from the hearts of kids who are no longer buying your lies. Listen as they proclaim the word of God in their schools. Listen as they lead their friends to the King. Listen as they pour out their souls to youth leaders who are sold out to the Master. And listen to the voice of their leaders interceding for them. Prayers are bombarding the heavens on their behalf and are keeping your demons at bay.

So look, listen, and count your days, for they are numbered.

One last thing, Satan. You better shore up the walls of your kingdom.

I'm getting ready to pray. ♡

Resources from Youth Specialties

Professional Resources

Administration, Publicity, & Fundraising (Ideas Library)

Developing Student Leaders

Equipped to Serve: Volunteer Youth Worker Training Course

Help! I'm a Junior High Youth Worker!

Help! I'm a Small-Group Leader!

Help! I'm a Sunday School Teacher!

Help! I'm a Volunteer Youth Worker!

How to Expand Your Youth Ministry

How to Speak to Youth...and Keep Them Awake at the Same Time

Junior High Ministry (Updated & Expanded)

One Kid at a Time: Reaching Youth through Mentoring

Purpose-Driven Youth Ministry

So That's Why I Keep Doing This! 52 Devotional Stories for Youth Workers

A Youth Ministry Crash Course

The Youth Worker's Handbook to Family Ministry

Youth Ministry Programming

Camps, Retreats, Missions, & Service Ideas (Ideas Library)

Compassionate Kids: Practical Ways to Involve Your Students in Mission and Service

Creative Bible Lessons from the Old Testament

Creative Bible Lessons in John: Encounters with Jesus

Creative Bible Lessons in Romans: Faith on Fire!

Creative Bible Lessons on the Life of Christ

Creative Junior High Programs from A to Z, Vol. 1 (A-M)

Creative Junior High Programs from A to Z, Vol. 2 (N-Z)

Creative Meetings, Bible Lessons, & Worship Ideas (Ideas Library)

Crowd Breakers & Mixers (Ideas Library)

Drama, Skits, & Sketches (Ideas Library)

Dramatic Pauses

Facing Your Future: Graduating Youth Group with a Faith That Lasts

Games (Ideas Library)

Games 2 (Ideas Library)

Great Fundraising Ideas for Youth Groups

More Great Fundraising Ideas for Youth Groups

Great Retreats for Youth Groups

Greatest Skits on Earth

Greatest Skits on Earth, Vol. 2

Holiday Ideas (Ideas Library)

Hot Illustrations for Youth Talks

More Hot Illustrations for Youth Talks

Incredible Questionnaires for Youth Ministry

Junior High Game Nights

More Junior High Game Nights

Kickstarters: 101 Ingenious Intros to Just about Any Bible Lesson

Live the Life! Student Evangelism Training Kit

Memory Makers

Play It! Great Games for Groups

Play It Again! More Great Games for Groups

Special Events (Ideas Library)

Spontaneous Melodramas

Super Sketches for Youth Ministry

Teaching the Bible Creatively

What Would Jesus Do? Youth Leader's Kit

Wild Truth Bible Lessons

Wild Truth Bible Lessons 2

Worship Services for Youth Groups

Discussion Starters

Discussion & Lesson Starters (Ideas Library)

Discussion & Lesson Starters 2 (Ideas Library)

Get 'Em Talking

Keep 'Em Talking!

High School TalkSheets

More High School TalkSheets

High School TalkSheets: Psalms and Proverbs

Junior High TalkSheets

More Junior High TalkSheets

Junior High TalkSheets: Psalms and Proverbs

What If...? 450 Thought-Provoking Questions to Get Teenagers Talking, Laughing, and Thinking

Would You Rather...? 465 Provocative Questions to Get Teenagers Talking

Have You Ever...? 450 Intriguing Questions Guaranteed to Get Teenagers Talking

Clip Art

ArtSource Vols. 1-7 on CD-ROM

ArtSource Vol. 8—Stark Raving Clip Art

ArtSource Vol. 8 & Promo Kit on CD-ROM

Videos

EdgeTV

The Heart of Youth Ministry: A Morning with Mike Yaconelli

Next Time I Fall in Love Video Curriculum

Understanding Your Teenager Video Curriculum

Student Books

Grow For It Journal

Grow For It Journal through the Scriptures

What Would Jesus Do? Spiritual Challenge Journal

Wild Truth Journal for Junior Highers